MW01025953

MASTER TANG HÔI

Other Books by Thich Nhat Hanh

MASTER TANG HÔI

First Zen Teacher in Vietnam and China

Thich Nhat Hanh

Parallax Press
Berkeley, California

Parallax Press
P.O. Box 7355
Berkeley, California 94707
www.Parallax.org

Parallax Press is the publishing division of Unified Buddhist Church, Inc.

© 2001, by Unified Buddhist Church.
All Rights Reserved.
Printed in the United States of America.

This book is a translation of *Thien Su Tang Hôi* by Thich Nhat Hanh (Paris, France: An Tiem, 1998). Translated by Sr. Annabel Laity.

Cover calligraphy by Thich Nhat Hanh.
Cover design by Nguyen Thi Hop and Nguyen Dong.
Text design by Gopa Design.
Author photograph by David Rhode.

Library of Congress Cataloging-in-Publication Data
Nhât Hanh, Thích.
    Master Tang Hôi : first Zen teacher in Vietnam and China /
Thich Nhat Hanh.
        p. cm.
    ISBN 1-888375-13-2
    1. Tang Hôi, 3rd cent. 2. Priests, Buddhist — Vietnam
    — Biography. 3. Priests,
    Buddhist — China — Biography. I. Title.

BQ990.A5275 N43 2001
294.3'927'092 — dc21
[B]   2001036459

2 3 4 5 6 7 8 9 10 / 07 06 05 04 03 02

Contents

Part II

Appendices

Preface

THIS BOOK PRESENTS an overview of the life, work, and thought of Tang Hôi, the earliest known Buddhist meditation master of Vietnam. Tang Hôi was born three hundred years before the well-known Indian monk Bodhidharma went to China in the region that is now Vietnam. He is revered by Vietnamese Buddhists as the first patriarch of the Vietnamese Meditation school, and his life and work tell us much about the roots of Buddhism in Vietnam and southern China.

The history of Buddhism in Vietnam spans two thousand years — nearly as long as Buddhism itself has been in existence. Due to Vietnam's geographical location between India and China, Vietnamese culture and religion were enriched by these two great cultures. As the life of Tang Hôi shows, Vietnam was the fertile soil for a unique form of Buddhism synthesized from the teachings of both the early Buddhist Theravadin tradition and the later Mahayana.[1]

In this work we will study two of Tang Hôi's writings, both composed sometime before 229 C.E. The first is an essay, "The Way of Realizing Meditation," which is an extract from his work, *The Collect-*

---

1 Theravada is a broad term describing a school of Buddhism that arose about two hundred years after the Buddha's lifetime. *Thera* means "elder," and the Theravadin school became the orthodox tradition, preserving and upholding the original teachings of the Buddha as collected in the Pali Canon. At the same time there was another school called the Mahasanghika school, which formed the basis for the development of the Mahayana, the "Great Vehicle," two hundred years later. Mahayana Buddhism was a movement for the renewal of certain elements that seemed to have been lost from the original teachings of early Buddhism. For an overview of the development of Buddhism in India, see Thich Nhat Hanh, *The Heart of the Buddha's Teaching* (Berkeley, CA: Parallax Press, 1998), chap. 4.

ion on the Six Paramitas. The second is his Preface to the *Anapananu-smriti Sutra (Sutra on the Full Awareness of Breathing),* which was written in Jiaozhou, the ancient name of the region that encompassed present-day northern Vietnam. Tang Hôi's writings reveal to us how second- and third-century Vietnamese Buddhists practiced meditation, and how their practice of the teachings contained in the Theravadin sutras was infused with the spirit of Mahayana Buddhism.

The Introduction of this book presents the historical background of Buddhism in Vietnam and of the life and practice of Tang Hôi in Vietnam and China. Part I and Part II give the full text of two writings by Tang Hôi, "The Way of Realizing Meditation" and the Preface to the *Anapananusmriti Sutra.*

These writings, which describe the meditation practice of Tang Hôi, are followed by the author's commentary. Some additional writings by other authors that relate to the life and teachings of Tang Hôi are included in the appendices.

This book is a translation of *Thien Su Tang Hôi* by Thich Nhat Hanh (Paris, France: An Tiem, 1998), which was based on a series of Dharma talks given by Thich Nhat Hanh during the 1994–95 winter retreat at Plum Village, the practice center where he lives in southwestern France. In presenting this material to students of Buddhism, he hopes to convey the richness of Vietnamese Buddhism and the remarkable contribution of Tang Hôi to the foundation and development of the Buddhist tradition in Vietnam.

Introduction: The Life and Practice of Tang Hôi in Vietnam and China

THE ANCIENT KINGDOMS OF VIETNAM

In order to understand how Buddhism took root in Vietnam, we need to know something about its early history and language as well as the influx of cultural and religious influences it received from the two great civilizations to its west and north, India and China.

The language of Vietnam is classified as Austroasiatic. There is archaeological evidence dating back to the end of the third millennium B.C.E. of a people of Austroasiatic origin living in what is now northern Vietnam. The earliest written historical records preserved by the Vietnamese people date from the seventh century B.C.E., the time when what was to become the nation of Vietnam was beginning to form. At that time the civilization of northern Vietnam was known as Van Lang (*van* means beautiful, and *lang* means kind and healing, like a good doctor). The ruling house of Van Lang was called Hong Bang, which means a kind of huge bird.

Legends are another form of recorded history, and those dating from the time of the Hong Bang kings reflect how this period was formative for Vietnamese culture. Among these legends are many well-known and well-loved Vietnamese stories, such as the tale of the earth and sky cakes, the round cake and the square cake, and the story of betelnut.[1]

Toward the end of the third century B.C.E., the Van Lang kingdom weakened and it was invaded by the neighboring kingdom of Thuc.

---

1 See Thich Nhat Hanh's collection of Vietnamese folktales, *A Taste of Earth and Other Legends of Vietnam* (Berkeley, CA: Parallax Press, 1993).

The exact location of the historical region of Thuc has not been determined, but it was likely north of Van Lang in what is now southern China. The Thuc and Van Lang kingdoms together formed a country called Au Lac, whose ruling house was called Thuc. The word *au* may stand for Au Co, a goddess who took the form of a bird; *lac* is also the name for a kind of bird. Many legends about Au Lac have also been preserved in Vietnamese tradition.[2] The culture that had begun to take shape in Van Lang continued to dominate in Au Lac and was further influenced by Indian civilization, whose reach extended across South and Southeast Asia.

In 179 B.C.E. Au Lac became part of Nam Viet (Chinese: Nan Yueh), which comprised an area from southern China to present-day northern Vietnam as far south as Hue. Hue sits nearly in the middle of present-day Vietnam, and it has long been considered the midpoint between north and south Vietnam. From the time Au Lac became Nam Viet, Vietnamese civilization, as it continued to develop in the north, began to be heavily influenced by Chinese culture.

About fifty years later, in 111 B.C.E. the Han Empire—the ethnic and political foundation of China—attained suzerainty over Nam Viet. The region encompassing what we know today as northern Vietnam was given the Chinese name Jiaozhou. The region of Jiaozhou was vast—the provinces of Guangdong, Guangxi, and the island of Hainan in China were part of it, as well as all of northern Vietnam. The capital of Jiaozhou was Luy Lau (present-day Thuan Thanh in northern Vietnam), a seaport in the province of Bac Ninh, an area considered by many scholars to be the cradle of Vietnamese civilization.

The literal meaning of *jiao* is "connection"; *zhou* means "place."[3] The name Jiaozhou reflects the fact that at that time, the land of Vietnam was the meeting place of two great cultures, those of India and China. In the first and second centuries C.E., Jiaozhou was mostly

2 See Thich Nhat Hanh, *A Taste of Earth,* Part One: "Beginnings."
3 Some Vietnamese believe that the word *jiao* means "dragon." This is because Vietnamese people in former times identified themselves as "descendants of the dragon."

influenced by Indian culture. Later on, due to its colonization by the Han Empire, Chinese culture came to be the predominant influence in Vietnam. Yet even though Jiaozhou was a colony of southern China for nearly a thousand years, from 111 B.C.E. until 939 C.E., it was never completely Sinicized. Vietnamese culture remains a unique form—bearing the influences of China and India, but standing in its own right.

Many people continue to refer to the countries of Laos, Kampuchea (Cambodia), and Vietnam collectively by the old colonial term, "Indochina." This name also reflects the fact that it was in this region where the cultural influences of India and China met. There is no reason why Vietnam today should not continue to play the role of a place where many cultures can come into contact with each other. If the Vietnamese people can offer their country as a place for diverse cultures and traditions to meet, they will be continuing the tradition of their ancestors and contributing to the enrichment of many different cultures—including their own.

Throughout its history, there have been many times when Vietnam has wished to reclaim some of its traditional lands. After the Han Empire colonized Jiaozhou in the second century B.C.E., the Vietnamese people staged many uprisings in the attempt to regain independence, but they were only briefly successful. In 40 C.E. two sisters, Trung Trac and Trung Nhi, led a revolution and an occupation army. The two sisters were able to establish an independent country for three years before it was again overrun by Han forces.

Colonization by the Han Empire brought a significant infiltration of Chinese culture into Vietnam. Two scholarly prefects, Xi Guang, prefect of Jiaozhou from 1–5 C.E., and Ren Yan, prefect of the territory that stretched from northern Vietnam to what is now Hue, devoted themselves to teaching the Chinese language to the people of Jiaozhou. Xi Guang and Ren Yan had the best interests of the people of Jiaozhou at heart. They introduced Chinese methods of rice cultivation, as well as Chinese social traditions such as engagement, marriage, and funeral ceremonies. Before this time, the people of Jiaozhou followed Indian customs for these rites of passage.

In 229 C.E. the Han dynasty was overthrown by the Wu dynasty in China. This period is known as the era of the Three Nations. The former Han Empire was divided into three parts: the region in the north, called Bei Wei; the southern region, called Dong Wu; and the area in the west, called Xi Chu. Jiaozhou lay in the south and belonged to Dong Wu. The capital of Jiaozhou was transferred from its former site at Luy Lau to Jianye in Peng Cheng.

The Arrival of Buddhism from India

Buddhism was first introduced to Vietnam from India via the sea trade routes, beginning around the first century C.E. Many people think that Buddhism came to Vietnam through China, but in fact it arrived first in Vietnam from India and was subsequently introduced to southern China from Vietnam.

Two renowned Mahayana Buddhist centers, Amaravati and Nagarjunakonda, established in the third century B.C.E., were located on the southern shores of eastern India. Monks and merchants traveling on the ships that plied the trade routes between India and the countries of Southeast Asia brought Buddhism to Vietnam from these Mahayana Buddhist centers on India's eastern seaboard. Over the next century, Buddhist scholars and monks continued to come to Vietnam from India, traveling with traders.

At that time India's trade with the Roman Empire was booming. Goods such as cinnamon, pepper, and silk were in high demand in the West. Indian merchants, unable to procure sufficient amounts of these goods in India, relied on trade with Southeast Asia. Each year the merchants waited for the season of the southeasterly winds to set out to sea in the direction of Vietnam. Their first port of call was Luy Lau, the capital of Jiaozhou. On arrival in Luy Lau, they stayed for several months to buy and sell merchandise. They then had to wait another six months until the winds were blowing in the right direction for the return journey to India.

During their stay in countries such as Vietnam, Buddhist Indian traders and the monks who accompanied them continued to practice Buddhism. This is how the Vietnamese people first learned about Buddhism. Frequently when making these dangerous journeys, the Indian merchants brought with them tiny *stupas* symbolizing relics of the Buddha. They lit sticks of incense, burned sandalwood, and recited sutras and Buddhist teachings such as the Three Refuges and the Five Mindfulness Trainings.[4] They also brought with them the Indian calendar, astronomical system, legends, medicines, and healing practices, all of which were adopted by the Vietnamese.

Merchants often invited monks to travel with them in order to ensure a safe journey under the protection of the Buddha. This practice still occurs in our own time. Refugees from Vietnam in the 1970s and '80s, the "boat people," often asked a monk or a nun to travel with them when they set out on their dangerous journeys. So one reason why there were a number of Indian monks coming to Vietnam to practice and teach was because they accompanied merchants there. Another reason, however, was that Mahayana Buddhists had a missionary spirit and wanted to bring the teachings of the Buddha to far-off places.

Monks who arrived in Luy Lau from India by sea and then stayed on taught Sanskrit to local monks. Indian monks who took up residence in Luy Lau established a very important community of practice there. Because Chinese was commonly used in Jiaozhou, monks and laypeople began to translate Sanskrit sutras into Chinese. By the third century C.E. at least fifteen sutras had been translated into Chinese in Luy Lau.

In Jiaozhou at that time many elements of Indian culture were still prevalent, so Indian monks arriving there felt at home. Some monks stayed in Luy Lau for a year and then returned to India, but others remained longer. Some merchants, too, decided to stay on, finding the new land an agreeable place to live. In fact, Tang Hôi's father was

4 For a discussion of these basic Buddhist teachings, see Thich Nhat Hanh, *The Heart of the Buddha's Teaching,* chaps. 13 and 21; and Thich Nhat Hanh, *For a Future to Be Possible: Commentaries on the Five Mindfulness Trainings,* Revised Edition (Berkeley, CA: Parallax Press, 1988).

a trader from India who stayed on in Jiaozhou and married the Vietnamese woman who was to become Tang Hôi's mother.

When Buddhism arrived in Jiaozhou it found ready acceptance from ordinary people. Confucianism and Taoism—traditions from China—had only just begun to be practiced in the region and had not yet become firmly established there. Han intellectuals would later maintain that Taoism and Confucianism were the only true paths and that all other paths were false. However, this narrow point of view did not yet exist in Jiaozhou when Buddhism was introduced there. In contrast, when Buddhism was introduced into China it first had to gain acceptance from the Taoist and Confucian intellectual elite, and only then was it allowed to filter down to common people. In Jiaozhou, Buddhism went directly to people of all walks of life.

By the late second to early third centuries c.e., the Han Empire had begun to unravel. This was a time of great social and political upheaval in China. Brigands raided the Han capital at Luoyang, and many people fled south to Jiaozhou as refugees. The district governor of Jiaozhou at that time, Shi Xie (b. 137 c.e.),[5] was a very talented scholar who was instrumental in enriching the culture of Jiaozhou by promoting Chinese studies and culture. His three brothers, who were prefects of different parts of Giao Châu, skillfully preserved the peace in Jiaozhou. So as the Han Empire began to collapse, many people migrated south to Jiaozhou, looking for a secure place to live. Many of those who came to Luy Lau were intellectuals, students of Taoism and Confucianism. For this reason Buddhism needed to be presented to them in a skillful way.

Among the refugees from China was a Taoist named Mouzi (b. 165 c.e.). While he was living in Luoyang, the Han capital, Mouzi knew nothing of Buddhism. When he was in his twenties he fled to Jiaozhou as a refugee, along with his mother. Mouzi had received a sound education based in Confucian and Taoist studies. Because of this training he was able to understand Buddhism very quickly and

---

5 Shi Xie (Vietnamese: Si Nhiep) served as governor of Jiaozhou from 187–226 c.e. and was a supporter of Buddhism.

discuss religious matters with the Chinese intellectuals who had come to Jiaozhou. Taking the Buddhist view in debate, he asked questions about the basic Confucian texts *The Four Books* and *The Five Classics*,[6] and about Confucianism and Taoism in general. The Chinese intellectuals were not able to defeat him in debate, yet they continued to hold that Taoism and Confucianism were lofty spiritual paths, while Buddhism was the path of barbarians. In response Mouzi said, "Do not say that. Buddhism is a very lofty spiritual path."

Mouzi developed a way of teaching that helped the Confucian and Taoist refugees from Han China understand Buddhism. He wrote a book called *Dispelling Doubts*,[7] which was a response to the various questions about Buddhism raised by the Confucian and Taoist intelligentsia. The first book on Buddhism written in Chinese, it was composed in Luy Lau in the second century C.E. As its title indicates, *Dispelling Doubts* was intended to remove the doubts people had about Buddhism. The final sentence in the book says that after people had heard Mouzi's explication of Buddhism, they thanked him and requested to receive the Five Mindfulness Trainings. Since in those days laypeople could not transmit the Five Mindfulness Trainings, we can infer from this that Mouzi was a monk. His preface to *Dispelling Doubts* is presented in Appendix One. This text tells us something about how Buddhism was taught and practiced in Vietnam in the second century.

Bhikshus (fully-ordained monks) in Jiaozhou received the 250 precepts of the Ten-Part Vinaya of the Sarvastivada school.[8] All Vietnamese monks practiced in the Mahayana tradition and in addition

6 *The Four Books* include *The Great Learning, The Confucian Analects, The Doctrine of the Mean*, and *Mencius. The Five Classics* include *The Book of Changes, The Book of Odes, The Book of Records, The Book of Ceremonies,* and *The Book of the Seasons.*
7 This work, *Lihoulun* in the Chinese Canon, has been translated into French by Paul Pelliot, *Meou Tseou ou les Doutes Levés;* and English by John P. Keenan, *How Master Mou Removes Our Doubts: A Reader-Response Study and Translation of the Mou-tzu Li-huo Lun* (Ithaca, NY: SUNY Press, 1994).
8 Each Indian school of Buddhism practiced a slightly different version of the bhikshu precepts. Modern-day Vietnamese monks receive the precepts of the Four-Part Vinaya of the Dharmagupta school.

were vegetarian. At that time there was not yet a community of fully-ordained nuns. The monks dressed in the manner of present-day monks in Thailand and Sri Lanka, in saffron-colored robes, since the gray, brown, and black robes we find today in China and Vietnam were not yet worn.

Historical evidence suggests that the people of Jiaozhou already used the term *But* (pronounced "bood") for Buddha in the second to third centuries c.e. Buddhist practitioners recited the Three Refuges and the Five Mindfulness Trainings and praised the Three Jewels (Buddha, Dharma, and Sangha) in Sanskrit. These recitations may also have been translated into Vietnamese. Monks studied and applied Theravadin meditation sutras, but they did so in the spirit of the Mahayana. The teachings of Tang Hôi are clear evidence of this synthesis. Tang Hôi dedicates two works to the Six *Paramitas,*[9] a Mahayana doctrine. But the practice as he writes about it has many features that can best be described as Theravadin in nature. These two works, *The Collection on the Six Paramitas* and *The Essence of the Six Paramitas,* were composed as teaching materials for the meditation center in Luy Lau.

THE THREE BUDDHIST CENTERS OF THE HAN ERA

In addition to the center in Luy Lau, there were two Buddhist centers in China, one in the Han capital, Luoyang, and one in Peng Cheng. Of the three, the Luy Lau Buddhist center was the most established and flourishing. At Luy Lau there were as many as five hundred ordained monks of Vietnamese descent, along with monks from India who had resettled in Jiaozhou. However, only a few visiting monks

---

9 The paramitas (perfections) are the six virtues that when cultivated take us to the shore of liberation. They are giving *(dana),* mindfulness trainings *(shila),* inclusiveness *(kshanti),* energy *(virya),* meditation *(dhyana),* and perfect understanding *(prajña).* For more on the paramitas, see Thich Nhat Hanh, *The Heart of the Buddha's Teaching,* chap. 25.

from India lived in the Chinese centers, and there were no monks of Chinese descent. This was because in the Han Empire it was forbidden for a Chinese person to ordain as a Buddhist monk.

The fact that the second-century Han refugee Mouzi studied Buddhism and wrote the first Chinese book on Buddhism in Luy Lau reflects how strong the Buddhist community of practice there was at that time. Later in the third century, Tang Hôi studied and translated in Luy Lau, further evidence that it remained a flourishing and important center of Buddhism. Tang Hôi's center in Luy Lau, which may have been in Dharma Cloud Temple (today known as Dau Temple), was located near the offices of the Chinese governor of Jiaozhou, Shi Xie. Dharma Cloud Temple was a major center of Buddhist meditation practice from its inception in the third century to the Ly dynasty (eleventh century), even though after 229 Luy Lau was no longer the capital of Jiaozhou.

According to recent research, it appears likely that the Luy Lau center was the starting point for the establishment of the Peng Cheng center, and in turn the Peng Cheng center was the starting point for the establishment of the Luoyang center. In this way, Buddhism became established in southern China from the strong roots of the Vietnamese tradition.

JIAOZHOU: THE FIRST HOME OF CHINESE BUDDHISM

Chinese historical records state that Buddhism first came to the Han Empire in the reign of King Han Mingdi (r. 75–58 B.C.E.), and that King Han Wandi (r. 147–167 C.E.) had altars both for Lao Tzu and for the Buddha in his palace temple. Part of the record is based on a legend about King Han Mingdi, in which he dreamed of a golden figure flying in front of the palace. When the king asked his advisors to interpret the dream, they told him that in the west there was a religious leader called Buddha and the golden figure he had seen in his dream was this Buddha. Because of this dream, the king sent a party to India via the land route, ordering them to bring back Buddhist sutras. After many years of arduous travel, the only sutra the party was able to acquire was the *Sutra of Forty-Two Chapters,* which they brought back and left in White Horse Temple.

Modern scholars no longer accept such legends about the origins of Buddhism in Luoyang as historical truth. It is hardly likely that merely on the basis of a dream a ruler would send a delegation on such a dangerous and difficult journey. Also, if the mandarins were able to identify the golden person in the dream as the Buddha, an Indian religious leader, this would have meant that the people of the region already knew about the Buddha.

It is more likely that Buddhism first came to Luoyang from Peng Cheng sometime in the first century C.E. Another legend, about a certain Chu Nang Ying, is connected with the founding of Xu Chang Temple in Luoyang. In 65 C.E. King Han Mingdi decreed that citizens who believed they had committed a crime against the state could redeem themselves by paying a tribute of gold, silver, or rolls of silk. Chu Nang Ying, one of the king's attendants, believing that he was unworthy even though he had not committed any crime, offered two rolls of silk. The king said to him, "You have not done anything wrong. On the contrary, you are someone who is worthy of our confidence. On the one hand you have studied the teachings of Lao Tzu, and on the other hand you have respect for the compassion of the Buddha."

Chu Nang Ying, encouraged by the king's words, undertook a ceremony of repentance, became vegetarian for three months, and organized offerings for the visiting Indian monks and laypeople. Chu Nang Ying lived in Peng Cheng. Whenever he went to Luoyang, he stayed at the house of his maternal cousin, Xu Chang. Later on the cousin's house was given as an offering and became Xu Chang Temple. According to this account, Chu Nang Ying was responsible for establishing at least one Buddhist center in Luoyang, modeled on the Buddhist center in Peng Cheng.

Scholars speculate about the route Buddhism followed into China.

According to the Chinese historical record, *The Book of the Later Han*, and research by Chinese scholars, it was possible to go from Luy Lau to Peng Cheng either by sea or land. The land route from Luoyang, the capital of the Han Empire, to India was much more difficult and dangerous than the sea route, although going by sea was a much longer journey. We know that Buddhism went from India by sea to Jiaozhou. Indian monks would have arrived at Luy Lau because it was the first port of call. From Luy Lau in Bac Ninh the route passed through Guangxi to Guangdong, and then went north to Peng Cheng, which lies on the route between Luy Lau and Luoyang. This is the route Tang Hôi took when he left Jiaozhou in the first half of the third century and went to Wu to practice and teach the Dharma, as well as the route many Indian monks had taken before him.

Biographies of High Monks,[10] a Chinese collection of biographies of eminent monks compiled by Master Huy Hao (496–553 C.E.), tells us that when Tang Hôi went to Jianye, the capital of Wu, in 247, he was the first Buddhist monk the people of that region had ever seen. After being converted to Buddhism by Tang Hôi, the Wu king Sun Quan had a temple built for him. It was originally called Buddha's Center and was later given the name First Temple, indicating that it was the first Buddhist temple in the land of Wu. From this we can surmise that the first Buddhist center in southern China was established by Tang Hôi and his Sangha from northern Vietnam.

THE LIFE OF TANG HÔI

Although there is no record of the date of Tang Hôi's birth, it is likely that he was born sometime in the first decade of the third century. The date of his death has been recorded as 280 C.E. His father was of Sogdian descent. Sogdia was a province in Central Asia to the northwest of the modern subcontinent of India, in what is now Uzbekistan.

10 *Kao-seng-ch'uan, Taisho* 2059. See Appendix Two for an excerpt on Tang Hôi from *Biographies of High Monks*.

His mother was a native of Jiaozhou (Vietnam). When Tang Hôi was only ten years old both his parents passed away, and he was accepted in a local temple as a young novice. We do not know the name of the monastery in which Tang Hôi studied and practiced, but we do know that it was in Luy Lau, the capital of Jiaozhou, in the province of Bac Ninh in what is now northern Vietnam. In the temple he studied the Buddhist sutras in Sanskrit and also learned Chinese.

By the time Tang Hôi had come of age and received bhikshu (monk) ordination,[11] he was well acquainted not only with Buddhism but also with Confucian and Taoist thought, which Buddhist monks in Vietnam at that time also studied. He became proficient in the sciences of divination,[12] astronomy, and geomancy, traditional skills taught in the Chinese system. He had studied and could quote long passages from Confucian works such as *The Four Books* and *The Five Classics*. Since many people would have been more familiar with these Chinese works than with Buddhist texts, teachers of Buddhism in those days typically drew from these books.

Tang Hôi not only lost his parents at an early age, he also lost three of his primary teachers in the monastery. In his Preface to the *Anapananusmriti Sutra* he writes, "I, Tang Hôi, had hardly reached the age when I could carry wood, when my mother and father passed away. My three ordination teachers, one after the other, also passed away." Though he was saddened by these losses, Tang Hôi was determined to practice and devote his life to helping others practice. He went on to establish a major practice center in Luy Lau, which may have been in Dharma Cloud Temple, where a large community of Vietnamese monks lived and practiced Buddhism under his guidance.

Under Han rule, it was forbidden for people to ordain as Buddhist monks. However, because Jiaozhou was such a remote part of the

11 The full ordination of a Buddhist monk, in which he undertakes the practice of the 250 precepts.

12 Divination here means the ancient Chinese system of the *I-Ching,* which utilizes an interpretation of the eight trigrams and the five elements (metal, wood, water, fire, and earth) to gain insight into the possible good or bad fortune that may accrue to people. Divination was one of the traditional studies of a Confucian education in Han China.

Han Empire—eighteen hundred miles from the capital at Luoyang —Buddhists were able to maintain a monastic Sangha comprised of local monks and Indian monks who had taken up residence in Luy Lau. In Tang Hôi's center, Buddhist scriptures were translated from Sanskrit into Chinese. Laypeople who came to Jiaozhou from the Han capital were also actively involved in translation work. Among them were Chen Hui and Pi Ye, lay disciples of Meditation Master An Shi Gao, who lived in Luoyang.

An Shi Gao was born a prince in Parthia, an ancient kingdom in present-day northeast Iran. Instead of succeeding his father to the throne, he chose to devote his life to Buddhist studies and practice. Among the sutras he translated in Luoyang are a number concerning meditation practice, including the *Anapananusmriti Sutra* and the *Skandha-dhatu-ayatana Sutra*. *Biographies of High Monks* mentions that An Shi Gao spent time in Jiaozhou. There is evidence that he arrived from Parthia by sea and arrived in Jiaozhou before he went north to Luoyang.

Though An Shi Gao did not have monastic disciples (due to the prohibition against Han people becoming monks), he did have several lay disciples who helped him with his translation work. An Shi Gao was well-versed in Sanskrit, but he relied on his Chinese lay disciples for the Chinese translation. Two of his lay disciples, Chen Hui and Pi Ye, went south as refugees to Jiaozhou, bringing with them a number of An Shi Gao's translations, including the *Anapananusmriti Sutra*. There they met Tang Hôi. He invited them to form a committee with him to translate and write commentaries on Buddhist sutras at Dharma Cloud Temple in Luy Lau. Layman Chen Hui wrote a commentary on the *Anapananusmriti Sutra* and gave it to Tang Hôi to review. In his preface to the commentary, Tang Hôi writes, "The layman Chen Hui did the work of writing the commentary, and I just gave some assistance by polishing the text, adding a little here and taking away a little there."

A passage in *Biographies of High Monks* states that An Shi Gao, who lived in Luoyang, knew of Tang Hôi. When An Shi Gao passed away he left behind these words: "The person who will develop the path I have taught is Layman Chen Hui, and the person who will transmit the teachings to meditation students is Bhikshu Tang Hôi." This passage confirms that the two people to whom An Shi Gao entrusted the transmission of his work were Chen Hui and Tang Hôi.

Tang Hôi also tells us in his Preface to the *Anapananusmriti Sutra*, "There is a bodhisattva who goes by the name of An Qing, whose title is Shi Gao. He was once heir to the throne of Parthia. After he abdicated in favor of his uncle, he came to this country. He traveled to many places and finally he came to the capital." These words establish that Tang Hôi's preface to the sutra was written before the fall of the Han dynasty in 229 C.E., because An Shi Gao went to Luoyang. After the fall of the Han Empire to the Wu dynasty, China was divided into three kingdoms. Jiaozhou belonged to the kingdom called Dong Wu and the capital of Dong Wu was not Luoyang but Jianye. We know that Tang Hôi wrote the preface to this sutra in Vietnam, because he did not travel to southern China until 247 C.E.

In teaching Buddhist meditation, Tang Hôi drew from basic meditation sutras such as the *Anapananusmriti*, the *Skandha-dhatu-ayatana*,[13] the *Ugradatta-paripriccha*, *The Tree of the Bodhisattva Path*,[14] the *Smrtyupasthana*, and the *Sutra of Forty-Two Chapters,* as well as Mahayana sutras such as the *Prajñaparamita in Eight Thousand Lines*,[15] and *The Collection on the Six Paramitas,* which he himself compiled.

TANG HÔI IN CHINA

After practicing and teaching in Luy Lau for some years, in 247 C.E. Tang Hôi went to Jianye, the Wu capital. There he built a small hut and settled in to practice.

At that time in Jianye there was only one Buddhist, a layman named Zhi Qian. Indian by birth, Zhi Qian was well-versed in the

13 *Yin Tche Jou, Taisho* 603.
14 *Tao Chou, Taisho* 532.
15 *Ba Qian Song Bore, Taisho* 229.

Buddhist sutras in both Chinese and Sanskrit. He had come to the northern Han Empire many years previously. When the political turmoil that accompanied the disintegration of the empire began, Zhi Qian had gone south to Dong Wu. The Wu king, Sun Quan, having heard that he was a man of learning, invited Zhi Qian to Jianye to help teach his son, Prince Sun Hao. Zhi Qian began translating sutras in 222 C.E. while living in the north, and he continued this work when he went south. Because he was a layperson, not a monk, he did not encounter hostility from the local people, who accepted him as a scholar and an intellectual.

When Tang Hôi arrived in Jianye, however, people were very suspicious of him. Rumors circulated about why a monk and meditation master from Jiaozhou should have come to Jiangzuo. (The region of Jiangzuo, literally, the "territory to the left of the river," occupied the area south of the Yangtze River.) Finally, King Wu Sun Quan summoned Tang Hôi to court. He questioned Tang Hôi and asked why he had come to Jianye. Because Tang Hôi was strong in his practice and a learned monk, he eventually was able to win over King Wu Sun Quan.

Tang Hôi established a practice center in Jianye, the First Temple. He organized ordination ceremonies there and taught the monks. For the first time in its history, natives of China were allowed to ordain and practice as Buddhist monks. After King Wu Sun Quan had authorized Tang Hôi to organize monastic ordination for natives of Wu, people in other parts of China also began to become Buddhist monks.

When Tang Hôi first came to Jianye, there were no ordained monastics at all in Dong Wu. So in order to convene the necessary number of monks required to transmit the precepts, he invited monks from Jiaozhou. To transmit the monastic precepts, Master Tang Hôi relied on a council of three teachers and seven witnesses. The three teachers were the *Upadhyaya,* the root teacher who presided over the ceremony; the *Sanghakarman* master, who was responsible for bringing the Sangha together to perform the ordination in the proper manner; and the *Dharmacarya,* who was in charge of instructing the ordinees in preparation for the ceremony. The witnesses were seven fully-ordained monks who were deemed well-established in their practice of the precepts.

The First Temple in Jianye was also called Buddha's Center. In the precincts of the First Temple a reliquary tope called the Ashoka Stupa was built, in which was enshrined a relic of the Buddha. Legend has it that the relic appeared magically as a result of the deep aspirations and power of concentration of Tang Hôi and his disciples. More likely, the relic had been given to Tang Hôi by his root teacher in Jiaozhou, and Tang Hôi took it with him when he went to live and teach in China. Other temples were later established in the region. *Biographies of High Monks* says, "From the time the First Temple was established, Buddhism prospered in the province of Jiangzuo."

But the "new" religion was not always supported by the rulers. When King Wu Sun Quan passed away he was succeeded by his son, Sun Hao, who proved to be more of an adversary to Tang Hôi than his father had been. Under the influence of the mandarins, who derided Buddhism as a religion of barbarians, Sun Hao did everything he could to oppose it. Nearly all Buddhist temples in the region were destroyed, although the king and the Wu mandarins did not dare to touch the First Temple because of its great prestige. Though the king did not destroy the temple he forced the name to be changed.

King Sun Hao summoned renowned intellectuals to challenge Tang Hôi and discredit his teachings. He ordered the intellectual Zhang Yu to the First Temple to debate Tang Hôi and force him into an impasse. Zhang Yu was fluent in the Taoist and Confucian texts and was known as a debater with considerable powers of eloquence. Many members of the Chinese intelligentsia from the capital were present at the debate, which went on from early morning until late at night.

Tang Hôi did not flinch. Because he had been educated not only in Buddhist scriptures but also in the Taoist and Confucian traditions, he was able to draw on his knowledge of *The Four Books* and *The Five*

Classics and responded to all of Zhang Yu's questions with ease. His interrogator was not able to fault a single word of Tang Hôi. Zhang Yu went to King Sun Hao and related what had happened at the debate: "Tang Hôi has a very clear mind. He is very eloquent and I did not have the capacity to contradict him. Your majesty, it would be best if you looked into the matter personally and decided what to do."

King Sun Hao summoned Tang Hôi to the palace. After questioning him and hearing him teach the Dharma, the king could only admire Tang Hôi, and from that time he stopped opposing him. Eventually, the teachings of Tang Hôi were able truly to penetrate his consciousness, and Sun Hao asked to take refuge and receive the Five Mindfulness Trainings. At that time the king gave permission for the First Temple to be extended and repaired, and for the temples that he had ordered destroyed to be rebuilt.

The First Temple continued to serve as an important center for the teaching and practice of the Buddhist teachings until the Minh era (fifteenth century). The name of the temple changed many times, but it remained the most important Dharma center in Jiangnan province. Many descendants of Tang Hôi's lineage trained there, including Meditation Master Seng You (445–518 c.e.), who came to study at the First Temple at a young age. Seng You was the first person to write about the life and work of Tang Hôi. This record is preserved in the *Collection from the Tripitaka*[16] as well as in *Biographies of High Monks*. After Seng You received the monastic precepts and completed his training, he continued to live at the First Temple to train disciples, teach, and write.

In 492, Master Ming Che came to the First Temple to train and he received the Ten-Part Vinaya from Seng You. He too stayed on to teach the Dharma there. The meditation masters who went on to establish the Dharma Eye school,[17] including Master Kuang Yi, Master Xuan Ze, and Master Fa An, all practiced, studied, and taught at

16 *Chu-San-Zang-Jij, Taisho* 2145.
17 This school was founded in the tenth century by Fayan, a disciple of the Sixth Patriarch of the Chinese Meditation (Ch'an) school, Hui-neng.

the First Temple. The Minh era King Cheng Zu had a splendid nine-story stupa built in the garden of the temple. Unfortunately, during the violent political upheaval in south China from 1851–1864, the temple, which was a continuation of the First Temple, was destroyed. Today not the slightest trace of this important historical site is left.

Tang Hôi:
First Patriarch of the Meditation School

In Chinese accounts, the Indian monk Bodhidharma, who came from India to China in the sixth century C.E., is considered the first patriarch of the meditation (dhyana, or *ch'an* in Chinese) tradition. Yet Bodhidharma did not himself record what he taught. Works such as *Essay on the Ultimate Contemplation (Jue Quan Lun)* and *The Six Doors of Mount Sao Shi* were written by others and later attributed to Bodhidharma.

The teachings of Tang Hôi are written in his own hand. They can be considered an exact record of what he taught in Jiaozhou and in the Wu province of Jiangzuo. There is textual evidence that Tang Hôi's *The Collection on the Six Paramitas,* which contains an essay called "The Way of Realizing Meditation," was completed before he wrote the Preface to the *Anapananusmriti Sutra*. The depth and clarity of Tang Hôi's expression of the Mahayana is more developed in the preface to the sutra than it is in "The Way of Realizing Meditation." We know that Tang Hôi's Preface to the *Anapananusmriti Sutra* was written before he left Jiaozhou for Dong Wu. Thus we can say with confidence that the Buddhist meditation tradition in southern China, in the region south of the Yangtze River (the Wu province of Jiangzuo), was first established and structured by the Vietnamese monk and meditation master Tang Hôi.

Tang Hôi is not only a patriarch of the Meditation school in Vietnam but, because he went to China to teach meditation in the mid-third century, he may also be considered an early patriarch of the

Meditation school in China.[18] Yet scholars of Buddhism very rarely mention Tang Hôi, and when they do, they do not speak of his teaching and practice of meditation. Much more research needs to be done on the teachings and the practice of Tang Hôi.

Students of the Vietnamese meditation tradition rely on *Flowers in the Garden of Meditation,* a book compiled in the fourteenth century.[19] The "flowers" of the title refer to the outstanding meditation masters of Vietnam. The authors of this book have recorded the names, careers, and teachings of Vietnamese meditation masters from three schools: the Vinitaruci,[20] the Vo Ngon Thong,[21] and the Shi Gao Tang.[22] According to this book, Tang Hôi established a meditation school in Vietnam, which continued until the Tran era (fourteenth century). After that the meditation school of Tang Hôi, along with other meditation schools, was gradually folded into the Bamboo Forest school which became the predominant school of the meditation tradition in Vietnam.

While in religious texts and other written materials a great deal had been recorded about Buddhism in India and China, there existed little documentation of the origins of Buddhism in Vietnam. In 1090, Phu Cam Linh Nhan, a queen of the Ly dynasty, invited all the monks in the capital to the palace to make offerings to them. When the monks had assembled for their midday meal, the queen rose and asked them: "Venerable monks, who among you can explain to me clearly what the roots of Buddhism in Vietnam are?"

Among the elders present that day was the monk Tri Khong. He responded to the queen's inquiry. He spoke about Mouzi of the second century and Tang Hôi of the third century. He also talked about

---

18 See *The Beginnings of the Meditation School of Vietnam,* Appendix Three.
19 *Thien Uyen Tap Anh,* translated into Vietnamese by Ngo Duc Tho and Nguyen Thuy Nga (Hanoi: Van Hoc Publishing House, 1990). An extract from this book appears in Appendix Four.
20 The Vinitaruci school was founded by an Indian meditation master of that name in the sixth century C.E. The school flourished until the early thirteenth century.
21 This school was founded by the Chinese master of the same name in the ninth century C.E. and continued until the late thirteenth century.
22 Founded in the eleventh century, it continued until the end of the twelfth century.

the monks Vinitaruci and Phap Hien. In 562 the Indian monk Vinitaruci came to Jiaozhou and stayed at the center in Luy Lau that Tang Hôi had established, Dharma Cloud Temple. There he met Quan Duyen, the temple's master of studies and director of meditation practice. One of Quan Duyen's outstanding disciples, Phap Hien, in time received Dharma transmission from Vinitaruci as well as from his master, Quan Duyen.

Master Tri Khong told the queen that Mouzi and Tang Hôi belonged to the Teachings school, whereas Vinitaruci and Phap Hien belonged to the Meditation school. The idea of these two schools, the Teachings school and the Meditation school, came from China. The Chinese tradition considered that those who belonged to the Teachings school concentrated on learning and practicing the recorded teachings (sutras) of the Buddha. Those who belonged to the Meditation school received direct instruction from a meditation master and practiced meditation without devoting time to study the words of the Buddha.

Masters of the Meditation school in China did not stress the teachings recorded in the sutras and commentaries. They taught that in order to meditate, it is not necessary to study the sutras: practitioners need only sit and breathe, they do not need to study the sutras, not even the *Sutra on the Mindfulness of Breathing*. Sometimes the Chinese masters even considered the instructions of the patriarchs of the Meditation school as more important than the teachings of the Buddha. This led to a different view of what a patriarch of the Meditation school was in the Chinese tradition.

Throughout the history of meditation practice in China, Korea, Japan, and Vietnam, people have viewed the Meditation school as different from the Teachings school. In Tri Khong's time, everyone in Vietnam was influenced by the idea that the roots of the Meditation school were in China. That is why Master Tri Khong did not look upon Tang Hôi as a patriarch of the Meditation school but saw him solely as a patriarch of the Teachings school. To entirely separate the two schools is not accurate, however.

The Indian monk Bodhidharma is considered part of the Meditation school, yet he is also said to have transmitted the *Lankavatara Sutra* to Patriarch Hue Kha. This sutra is a written teaching on Buddhist psychology and the meditative concentration of *Tathagatagarbha* — the original pure mind. Therefore to say that meditation practice is entirely divorced from the written teachings is not correct, and to say that the Teachings school only studies the sutras and does not practice meditation is also not correct. In the history of meditation there have been meditation masters who have maintained the link between the Meditation and the Teachings schools. We can see that Patriarch Tang Hôi followed that path. He practiced and taught meditation but continued to use the written teachings of the Buddha as the basis of his practice and teaching.

Tri Khong also said to the queen: "There was a time when King Sui Wendi in China said to the Chinese Dharma Master Tan Qian that he wanted to send a delegation to bring Buddhism to Jiaozhou in order to propagate the true teachings in that far-off place. This king was someone who had a very high respect for Buddhism and had sponsored the establishment of many temples in China as well as the practice of monastic Sanghas."

This story about Tan Qian and King Sui Wendi happened in the sixth century. Master Tan Qian replied to the king: "Your majesty, at the time when our country knew nothing about Buddhism, in Jiaozhou, Buddhism was already being practiced. At a time when in China we did not have any monks, there were monks in Jiaozhou already. At a time when we had no sutras there were already sutras in Jiaozhou. At that time there were about five hundred monks and fifteen sutras that had been translated from Sanskrit."

Master Tri Khong was a historian who was very well-educated and had studied many sources. He was able to respond eloquently when the queen asked about the origins of Buddhism in Vietnam, and so the queen asked the king to bestow on him the title of National Teacher Clear Eloquence (Thong Bien). So Tri Khong became Thong Bien. Master Thong Bien wrote down some of his thoughts on the history of Buddhism in Vietnam. This document was handed down to other meditation masters, namely Thuong Chieu, Than Nghi, and An Khong, and eventually became the work we know today as *Flowers in the Garden of Meditation.*[23]

THE CAREER OF TANG HÔI
AS A MEDITATION MASTER

Tang Hôi's career as a meditation master had a far-reaching effect. Thanks to his writings we know about the nature of his meditation practice in Luy Lau in Vietnam, as well as in the Jianye center in China that he possibly established. The principles on which he based his teaching of meditation are Mahayana. They have much in common with the principles of the *Avatamsaka Sutra*[24] and the Mahayana teachings of Buddhist psychology, although these two streams of Buddhism were not formulated until several hundred years later.

The foundations of the practice of meditation that Tang Hôi teaches—conscious breathing and mindfulness of the four establishments of body, feelings, mind, and phenomena, as well as other basic methods of contemplation—are drawn from the meditation sutras of early Buddhism. In this way, Tang Hôi's teaching combines the spirit of the Mahayana with the practical teachings of early Buddhism. And because they are based on his authentic experience of the practice, Tang Hôi's meditation teachings are very useful and are still applicable by students of meditation today.

We cannot underestimate the importance of Tang Hôi in the lineage of ancestral teachers of Buddhism. A *gatha* by Sun Chuo, an intellectual of Dong Wu, which was inscribed on the base of a statue of Tang Hôi,[25] reveals to us something of his character:

23 For more on Master Thong Bien, see Appendix Four.
24 Available in English as *The Flower Ornament Sutra: A Translation of the Avatamsaka Sutra,* translated by Thomas Cleary (Boulder, CO: Shambhala Publications, 1993).
25 This statue was destroyed along with the temple.

Noble silence and solitude
Was his path.
With the mind of a free person
And emotions unattached,
He brought a lamp to shine the way.
He was able to awaken people.
Overcoming all obstacles he went far,
Never caught in worldly things.

PART I:
The Way of Realizing Meditation

In this section the full text of "The Way of Realizing Meditation" by Tang Hôi is presented, followed by the author's commentary. The essay is extracted from *The Collection on the Six Paramitas (Taisho 152)*, which was composed by Tang Hôi. In *The Collection on the Six Paramitas*, Tang Hôi gathered hundreds of stories on the life of the Buddha and the former lives of the Buddha from the sutras and divided them into six chapters. Every chapter in the collection contains stories that relate to each of the Six Paramitas. At the beginning of each chapter, Tang Hôi wrote an introductory essay. "The Way of Realizing Meditation" is an essay that he wrote at the beginning of the chapter on meditation ("The Unlimited Virtue of Meditative Concentration That Takes Us to the Other Shore"). In this essay, Tang Hôi combines the Mahayana concepts of the bodhisattva and the Six Paramitas with the four meditative concentrations from the Theravada.

The Way of Realizing Meditation

By Tang Hôi

(from *The Collection on the Six Paramitas*)

Translated from Chinese into Vietnamese by Thich Nhat Hanh

Translated into English by Sr. Annabel Laity

WHAT IS THE BOUNDLESS VIRTUE of meditative concentration that can take us to the other shore? It is making our mind upright again. We devote our mind to one object and accumulate all the wholesome formations. We use these wholesome mental formations to eliminate the impurities that are still clinging to our mind. That is the boundless virtue of meditation that takes us to the other shore.

There are four meditative concentrations. The practice of the first meditative concentration is to eliminate craving and the going awry that are brought about by the five kinds of clinging. This clinging takes place when the eyes are in contact with form, the ears are in contact with sound, the nose is in contact with scent, the tongue with taste, the body with pleasant touch, and the mind gives rise to desire. Those who intend to realize the path at the very least should distance themselves from the sense desires. They also need to destroy the Five Hindrances of craving, anger, dullness, agitation and regret, and doubt. Doubt means doubt about the existence of the path of practice, the existence of the Buddha, and the existence of the teachings of the Buddha.

When the whole mind, including the conscious mind and the unconscious store consciousness, has been cleared of all impurities, it is very bright. It is able to see the truth, and it reaches a state where there is nothing it does not understand. At that point the gods, the *nagas*,[1] and the spirits are no longer able to deceive the practitioner. Someone who realizes the first meditative concentration is like a person who has managed to escape from ten different enemies. She is alone on a high mountain, and, since no one knows where she is, she no longer has any reason to be afraid. When someone is able to leave behind the sense desires, she feels pure and clear within, and her mind is at rest. When the first meditative concentration has been realized, the practitioner takes another step in the direction of the second meditative concentration.

Someone who realizes the second meditative concentration is like a person who has managed to escape from his enemies. Although he has gone deep into the mountains, he still has a little anxiety that those enemies could come and find him. So he wants to go deeper into the mountains to hide himself. Although the practitioner has left behind the five kinds of sensual desire and the Five Hindrances, he is still afraid that those enemies will come and find him and destroy his aspiration to be awakened.

When we realize the second meditative concentration, we leave all craving far behind, and it is no longer able to corrupt us. In the first meditative concentration, the wholesome mental formations and the unwholesome mental formations still oppose each other. The practitioner uses the wholesome mental formations to destroy the unwholesome ones, and, as the unwholesome ones retreat, the wholesome mental formations advance. In the second meditative concentration, the bliss of the first meditative concentration comes to an end. The practitioner no longer uses the method of destroying unwholesome mental formations by means of wholesome mental formations, and therefore the two elements of bliss and attachment to wholesomeness are no longer there. The ten unwholesome mental formations have come to an end and cease to manifest. There is nothing that could make them invade the practitioner's mind from the

---

1 A kind of serpent or dragon believed to have divine powers. They are said to support the Dharma when properly treated by people.

outside anymore. It is like a spring of water on a high mountain peak. The clear water in the bed of the spring does not come from streams that run into the spring from outside, nor is it brought in by the rain that the nagas cause to fall. This water comes from the heart of the spring. Just as the clear water fills the bed of the spring, so the wholesome mental formations flow out from within the practitioner's mind, and unwholesome mental formations are not produced by sense objects that enter the practitioner by way of the eyes, ears, nose, and tongue. The meditator who has restrained the mind in this way begins to go in the direction of the third meditative concentration.

In the third meditative concentration the practitioner is able to maintain right mindfulness very solidly. Ideas of wholesome and unwholesome are not able to agitate her. Her mind is as unmovable as Mount Sumeru. The wholesome mental formations are not produced outside the mind, and therefore the wholesome and the unwholesome are not able to invade the mind. The mind is like the stem and roots of a lotus flower lying on the bed of a lake. The bud of the lotus flower is still covered by the water and has not lifted itself above the surface. In the third meditative concentration the calm and clarity are like a lotus flower. All impurities have been eliminated, and the body and mind are at peace. When the mind has been mastered in such a way, the meditator begins to go in the direction of the fourth meditative concentration.

On reaching the fourth meditative concentration, the practitioner has wholly eliminated ideas of wholesome and unwholesome. The mind does not long for the wholesome and does not hold on to the unwholesome. The content of the mind is as bright and clear as lapis lazuli. It is like a princess who has bathed and rubbed herself with fragrant oils. All her clothes are new, and she is clean and fragrant. When the mind of the bodhisattva has become straight and upright after achieving the fourth meditative concentration, the impurities that make her mind unstable no longer have the power to hide her mind from her.

Just as a painter has the freedom to use whatever colors and forms she likes, or a potter can produce whatever vessels he likes out of clay, or a goldsmith according to his wishes can produce hundreds or thousands of different forms of skillfully made adornments, the bodhisattva who makes her mind calm and clear and realizes the fourth meditative concentration can do whatever she likes. She can fly or walk in space, travel under the water, appear in many bodies in different places, move through matter without it being an obstruction, appear and disappear at will, touch the sun and the moon, cause the earth and sky to tremble, see through matter, and hear sounds from afar. There is nothing she does not see or hear.

When his mind is concentrated and his observation is clear, the bodhisattva understands all things. He understands the state of things before the heavens, the earth, and living beings existed. He can know the minds of living beings in the ten directions in the present moment. He can know what has happened to them from when they were first conceived. He can see the cycle of birth and death of living beings: how they are born as humans or gods, and how they fall into the hell realms, the hungry ghost realms, and the animal realms. He sees how they undergo retribution for their wrongdoing when they have exhausted the merit of their virtuous actions, and how, when their misfortune has come to an end, they can again enjoy happiness. In short, nothing can happen near or far away that the bodhisattva does not know about. That is the effect of the fourth meditative concentration.

Someone who wants to realize the fruits of stream-enterer, once-returner, no-returner, and *arhatship* or the highest right awakening that is the wisdom of equalness of the Awakened One, has to realize the fourth meditative concentration. Once this has been attained, anything is possible. Just as all the animal, plant, and mineral species come from the earth, so the fruits of the practice, such as the five higher knowledges to the state of Tathagata, all come from success in the practice of the fourth meditative concentration. When people build, the earth is the place where they lay the foundations. So the fourth meditative concentration is the foundation for realization in the practice. The World-Honored One has taught: "Living beings, including the gods and the holy ones, however high their intelligence and wonderful their skills may be, if they do not practice what is written in the sutras, and they do not realize the concentration that eliminates the unwholesome states of mind, must still be ranked among those who are in a dream." If someone realizes awakened understanding and maintains the determination to be close to those who are suffering and to rescue them, that is the boundless virtue of meditative concentration that takes one to the other shore. The bodhisattva is determined to realize this.

In former times, the bhikshu, after taking the midday meal and bathing, went deep into the mountains and sat at the foot of a tree in meditation. He placed one hand on top of the other, inclined his head forward a little, established the silence of mindfulness, and with one-pointed mind stilled his thoughts, destroying the Five Hindrances from within his mind. Once the Five Hindrances are destroyed, the practitioner's mind becomes clear. The darkness retreats, and the light remains. He is able to meditate on and be mindful of human beings, gods, and living beings that creep, fly, move, or crawl. He feels love and compassion for these beings, because they do not have clear understanding and they continue to be caught in the Five Hindrances, so that the wholesome and wonderfully clear mind that they have cannot reveal itself.

When we are able to destroy the Five Hindrances, then the wholesome dharmas will prosper and increase. It is like when a poor person has been able to pay off all her old debts and begins to make a profit, so that every day she has a little more than she had the day before. She feels very happy. It is like a slave who has been given his freedom and the rights of citizenship. It is like when someone who has been seriously ill is healed, which makes all his relatives rejoice daily. It is like when someone who has committed a serious crime and been imprisoned is granted a reprieve and recovers his freedom. It is like when someone crosses the ocean with a cargo of precious jewels and, having passed through many difficulties, returns home to his family and feels tremendous joy. When the mind continues to hold on to the Five Hindrances, we suffer like these five people before they were liberated. A bhikshu who sees the truth and eliminates the Five Hindrances is like the ordinary person when she is able to be liberated from the five misfortunes recounted above. When the hindrances are made to retreat, then the light of the mind shines out. All the unwholesome mental formations are destroyed. The deep aspiration to be awakened prospers, and we realize the first meditative concentration.

To go from the first to the second meditative concentration, we need to practice three things: diligence, maintaining right mindfulness, and using the tool of looking deeply. With these three things, the practitioner will be successful in reaching the fourth meditative concentration. From the first meditative concentration, one rises to the second. On the basis of the second meditative concentration, one rises to the third. On the basis of the third meditative concentration, one rises to the fourth. The fourth meditative concentration is higher than the third. The third is higher than the second. The second is higher than the first.

In the first meditative concentration, the ten unwholesome mental formations retreat, and the five wholesome mental formations advance. What are the unwholesome mental formations? They are the five internal formations that arise when the eyes are in contact with form, the ears with sound, the nose with scent, the tongue with taste, the body with touch, plus the Five Hindrances talked about above. What are the five wholesome mental formations? They are initial thought, subsequent discursive thought, joy, happiness, and one-pointed mind. These five wholesome mental formations are present in the first meditative concentration. In the second meditative concentration, initial thought and subsequent discursive thought are no longer present. The mind is able to maintain the object of meditation. The wholesome mental formations manifest and are maintained from within. They do not come from outside through the eyes, ears, nose, and tongue. At this point, the ideas of wholesome and unwholesome no longer oppose each other. The mind dwells within itself, and within the mind there is only bliss and happiness. In the third meditative concentration, bliss is no longer there; the mind is directed toward purification and dwells peacefully in a deep silence. This is the state that the Buddha and the holy *arhats* call the capacity to destroy desire and purify the mind. Only now are the depths of the mind truly stable and at peace. When the fourth meditative concentration is reached, happiness is given up, and a concentration of deep silence is realized.

The obstacle to the first meditative concentration is the noise that the practitioner hears. The obstacle to the second meditative concentration is initial thinking and subsequent discursive thought. The obstacle to the third meditative concentration is bliss. The obstacle to the fourth meditative concentration is counting the breath. Therefore, in the first meditative concentration, we must put an end to all noise in order to give rise to the second meditative concentration. In the second meditative concentration, we put an end to initial thinking and subsequent discursive thought in order to give rise to the third meditative concentration. In the third meditative concentration, we put an end to bliss in order to give rise to the fourth meditative concentration. In the fourth meditative concentration, we stop counting the breath in order to realize the concentration of emptiness. This is how the bodhisattva practices with one-pointed mind to realize the boundless virtue of meditative concentration that takes us to the other shore.

There are many circumstances that are favorable to the bodhisattva's aspiration to be awakened and help her to achieve the state of inner silence and one-pointed mind, which makes it possible to have meditative concentration. For example, when bodhisattvas see an old person with white hair, loose teeth, and a body in a process of deterioration, they wake themselves up by remembering that their own body will be like that in the future. Because of that, they realize meditative concentration. When bodhisattvas see someone who is sick, afflicted in body and mind, their life at risk, and pain like a knife cutting into the flesh, they suffer and wake themselves up by thinking that their own body in time will be like that, and thus they realize meditative concentration.

The bodhisattvas see living beings die. The breath stops, the body grows cold, the consciousness leaves the body, the corpse grows rigid, and all loved ones are left behind. The corpse is taken out to a deserted place, and a couple of days later it becomes fetid. Hyenas and vultures come and eat it, insects and maggots are born inside it and consume it. Blood and a foul-smelling substance trickle out of the corpse onto the earth, and then the bones are scattered in different places. A leg bone is in one place, an arm bone in another, the skull and the teeth are somewhere else. Someone who practices awakening meditates that for as long as there is birth there is death; the life of a human being, like everything else, is like a magic display. When something is composed of different elements, it will decompose. When consciousness leaves the body, it decomposes. We cannot avoid death, and our very own body will also come to this state of decomposition. Seeing this, the bodhisattva feels compassion and makes her mind one-pointed in order to realize meditative concentration. The bodhisattva may see a corpse that has been lying for a long time, the bones have rotted and become dust and earth, and she contemplates deeply, telling herself: "My own body is like that." For that reason she realizes meditative concentration.

The bodhisattva hears about the fierce suffering of the blazing fires and boiling water in the hell realms, the long-lasting hunger and thirst of the hungry ghosts, and the pain of the animals who are slaughtered and cut into pieces to be food for human beings. Contemplating like this, the bodhisattva is startled and makes his mind one-pointed in order to realize meditative concentration. The bodhisattva sees a poor person dying of hunger or cold, or he sees a criminal sentenced to death by the king, and he meditates: "That person has fallen into misfortune because he does not practice the aspiration to be awakened. If I do not practice diligently I could also find myself in such a situation." Contemplating like that he makes his mind one-pointed in order to realize meditative concentration.

The bodhisattva meditates on the inside of her own body and sees the urge to urinate and defecate and the burning of fever. She sees that this body is impermanent and impure, and because of that she makes her mind one-pointed in order to realize meditative concentration.

The bodhisattva sees a year when the crops fail, the poor people are starving, and they rise up in revolt. This causes a war, and everywhere there are corpses. At this he feels compassion and thinks that if he did not practice to be awakened, he too would behave like that, and so he makes his mind one-pointed in order to realize meditative concentration.

The bodhisattva recognizes that as long as there is prosperity there must be decline, and that material riches do not last forever. She knows that, however young we are, it is certain that one day we will grow old and sick. When she sees that life passes as quickly as a flash of lightning, she is startled and makes her mind one-pointed in order to realize meditative concentration.

When the bodhisattva contemplates the incomparably wonderful signs of the Buddha's body, he knows that these signs are due to the purification of the practice over many lifetimes. For only then is a person able to tame the minds of living beings. Keeping this contemplation in his mind, great joy arises in him and, because of that, he makes his mind one-pointed in order to realize meditative concentration.

The bodhisattva contemplates on the deep and wonderful teachings of the Dharma and on the high level of pure practice of the *sramanas* and makes his mind one-pointed in order to realize meditative concentration. He makes a deep aspiration to use his body to realize awakening and to build up his virtue now and in the future and makes his mind one-pointed in order to realize meditative concentration.

Contemplating the desires of an ignorant person and the behavior that runs counter to the true teachings, she sees that these things not only bring about toil and suffering but also lead to further wrongdoing. Contemplating how human beings are born in the world of the gods because they observe the precepts and practice vegetarianism and as gods are able to enjoy an extremely long life span and happiness, the bodhisattva makes her mind one-pointed in order to realize meditative concentration.

When the bodhisattva receives the teachings of the Buddha, studies and experiences them, and is taught and instructed by the noble Sangha, her mind rejoices, and because of that she makes her mind one-pointed in order to realize meditative concentration.

Any of the species of living beings that come to be will pass away, and when there is passing away there is suffering. Contemplating like this, the bodhisattva gives rise to compassion and makes his mind one-pointed in order to realize meditative concentration. The nature of sentient beings is such that they cannot guarantee the survival of their own person. Every one of them has to go through processes of change. Someone who practices awakening has fear, knowing that when he passes away he could fall into paths of cruel suffering. Seeing that prosperity and honors, whether they are real or false, are all like a dream, the bodhisattva sees the importance of awakening and for that reason makes his mind one-pointed in order to realize meditative concentration.

When food goes into the mouth it seems to be fragrant and appetizing. But afterwards it is mixed with saliva and the digestive juices in the stomach and intestine, and finally it turns into excrement. Recollecting this, the bodhisattva is startled and makes her mind one-pointed in order to realize meditative concentration.

When an embryo is in the womb of its mother, at first it is like a soup that has jelled. Afterwards it gradually grows. As it grows from the thirtieth to the eighty-seventh day, it takes on the form of a body. The hour of birth is full of danger, and there is very little peace in it. After birth, whether the person is one year or ten years old, fifty years or one hundred years old, he is destined for death, and no one can escape that misfortune. Contemplating like that, the bodhisattva makes her mind one-pointed in order to realize meditative concentration. She meditates and sees that if things last they also disappear, and once someone has died we cannot find them anywhere. All three worlds are empty.[2] When the bodhisattva sees this, she no longer gives rise to craving or regret. When the bodhisattva thinks about and feels compassion for living beings who, because they have not met the Buddha or the teachings of the Buddha, are obscured by wrong desires and have not understood the truth of impermanence, she makes a deep aspiration to help them, and for that reason makes her mind one-pointed in order to realize meditative concentration.

A good mother always loves and cares for her child and keeps a close eye on her child. When the child goes out to play with other children and comes home covered in dust or mud, crying because he is hungry, his mother out of love carries him into the house, washes him clean, and gives him food. When the child is at peace and happy in body and mind, then the mother also feels content. She never has the heart to leave her child alone. Someone who practices awakening is the same. With a heart of love and compassion he directs his thoughts to guarding and protecting living beings like a good mother. He cares for people and for all species of creeping, crawling, flying, and moving things. He teaches everyone to respect the Buddha, to read the sutras, to be near the Sangha, to receive, observe, and practice the mindfulness trainings of the Buddha. He tells people how to leave behind the three unwholesome things, to recollect the three wholesome things, to say kind things, to do kind things in order not to have to fall again into realms of suffering, danger, and poverty, like the hell realms and the hungry ghost and animal realms. He also teaches them that although they may be enjoying peace and the reward for having done good things, they should remember that however great the good deeds we have done, if we allow our unwholesome mind to increase, sometime in the future we will fall again into the three lower realms. For that reason, honors and advantages can also be a calamity. Someone who practices awakening teaches others about the impermanent, suffering, and selfless nature of all that is. He wakes

2 The desire realm, the form realm, and the formless realm. The desire realm is the realm of most human beings. The form and formless realms are those of the gods and of meditators who have realized the four meditative concentrations.

them up and encourages them to practice these teachings in order that they may arrive at liberation and nirvana, just as a good mother embraces and protects her child.

The bodhisattva knows how to practice the sixteen methods of mindful breathing in order to make her mind one-pointed and to realize meditative concentration. What are these sixteen methods?

Breathing in and out a long breath, she knows she is breathing in and out a long breath.

Breathing in and out a short breath, she knows she is breathing in and out a short breath.

Breathing in and out and being aware of the body, she knows she is aware of the body.

Breathing in and out and calming the body, she knows she is calming the body.

Breathing in and out with a pleasant feeling, she knows she has a pleasant feeling.

Breathing in and out with an unpleasant feeling, she knows she has an unpleasant feeling.

Breathing in and out and calming the feeling, she knows she is calming the feeling.

Breathing in and out and not calming the feeling, she knows she is not calming the feeling.

Breathing in and out and feeling happy, she knows she is happy.

Breathing in and out and not feeling happy, she knows she is not happy.

Breathing in and out, she sees that all things are impermanent.

Breathing in and out, she sees that nothing can be grasped hold of.

Breathing in and out, she sees that there is no attachment in her mind.

Breathing in and out, she knows she is giving up her perceptions.

Breathing in and out, she knows she is giving up her idea of body and life span.

Breathing in and out, she knows she has not yet given up her idea of body and life span.

The practitioner should reflect deeply to see that only when something exists can it be grasped hold of. When something does not exist, it cannot be grasped hold of. The principle of impermanence is that, when there is birth, it will be followed by old age and death. Because consciousness is not destroyed, another body can then be formed. If we can realize birthlessness, there will not be old age and death. Contemplating like that, the bodhisattva makes her mind one-pointed in order to realize meditative concentration.

The bodhisattva observes life and death in the world with his own eyes and sees that it is a continuation of the twelve causes and results.[3] Contemplating like this he makes his mind one-pointed in order to realize meditative concentration.

The bodhisattva uses the five methods of meditating on the body. First, he meditates on the changes of the face. Second, he meditates on the changes between suffering and happiness. Third, he meditates on the changes of intention. Fourth, he meditates on the changes in the body. Fifth, he meditates on the changes between wholesome and unwholesome. These changes take place like a stream of flowing water, always following one after the other. Meditating like this, he

3 The twelve *nidanas:* ignorance gives rise to formations, formations give rise to consciousness, consciousness gives rise to mind/body, mind/body gives rise to the six sense organs and the six objects of the senses. The six sense organs and the six objects of the senses give rise to contact, contact gives rise to feelings, feelings give rise to craving, craving gives rise to grasping, grasping gives rise to becoming, becoming gives rise to birth, and birth gives rise to old age, death, and all subsequent suffering. For more on the nidanas, see Thich Nhat Hanh, *The Heart of the Buddha's Teaching,* chap. 27.

makes his mind one-pointed in order to realize meditative concentration.

How should the bodhisattva use meditative concentration in the right way? For example, when his eyes observe a dead person from the head down to the feet, his mind should contemplate deeply and note exactly what he sees. He should maintain this image at all times — when he is walking, standing, lying down, sitting, eating, drinking, or doing any one of ten thousand other things. He should maintain this meditation in his heart in order to consolidate his aspiration to be awakened, and then he will be able to nourish the object of his mindfulness in meditative concentration naturally and easily. It is like when someone takes a little rice from a pot with chopsticks to see if it is cooked. He only needs to take one grain and observe it. If that grain is cooked, then the whole pot of rice is cooked. Once the aspiration to be awakened is strong, then the whole mind will follow its direction quite naturally, as water follows water in a stream.

The bodhisattva needs diligently to direct the strength of her mindfulness upon one object. Constant thinking should come to a halt, and thought should be calm and clarified. If she goes on the right path like this, she can realize the fruit of arhatship and the attainment of cessation.[4]

Is it possible to attain the fruit of arhatship by practicing the four meditative concentrations? It is possible but not always so. How will the practice be successful, and how will the practice not be successful? In the first meditative concentration, there is still initial thinking, subsequent discursive thought, and bliss, and so awakening has not yet been realized. The heavens and the earth are impermanent, and space is something we cannot hold on to. Someone has to put an end to all the impurities within, be mindful of craving, and be mindful that craving is no longer there. When the mind is purified like that, then realization of arhatship is possible, whether it is during the second meditative concentration, the third meditative concentration, or the

4 This is a level of concentration where feelings and perceptions are transformed.

fourth meditative concentration. If the mind is still at the first meditative concentration, then it is not yet possible to realize the fruit of arhatship, and when the practitioner passes away she will be reborn in the seventh heaven where she will dwell for one lifetime. If the practitioner has realized the second meditative concentration, when she passes away she will be born in the eleventh heaven and will pass two lifetimes there. If the mind of the practitioner is established in the third meditative concentration, she will be born in the fifteenth heaven and will pass three lifetimes there. If her mind is established in the fourth meditative concentration, she will be born in the nineteenth heaven and will pass sixteen lifetimes there.

The bodhisattva who practices awakening meditates on the impure substances within the body and contemplates the hair, teeth, bones, marrow, ligaments, tears, mucous, saliva, brains, liver, lungs, intestines, heart, kidneys, blood, and urine. These impure elements are what make up our person. Our body is like a bag containing all kinds of grains. Someone who has good eyes and opens the bag can tell clearly which seed is which. Someone with understanding also looks at his body in the same way. Among the four species,[5] every species has a name, but within them we cannot find a self. With the eyes of nonattachment we can look deeply and see that they are empty by nature, and because of that we realize meditative concentration. The bodhisattva looks deeply and can distinguish the four elements in the body, which are earth, water, fire, and air. Hair of the head, hair of the body, teeth, bones, skin, flesh, and the five internal organs belong to the earth element. Tears, mucous, saliva, blood, pus, sweat, marrow, and urine belong to the water element. The heat in the body has the ability to digest food, and that is the element fire. The in-breath and the out-breath are the element air. It is like a butcher who slaughters an animal and divides it into four parts. He sees that there are four parts. When the bodhisattva looks deeply at his body, he can distinguish the four elements, seeing that this is the earth ele-

5 Species born from a womb, from an egg, from moisture, or spontaneously.

ment, this is the water element, this is the fire element, and this is the air element. Everything is just the four elements, and there is no separate self. The practitioner meditates like this until the mind is absolutely quiet, and then it can be one-pointed and realize meditative concentration.

The practitioner is aware of whether the breath is long or short, fast or slow, gross or subtle, and can distinguish the quality of her breathing as clearly as someone who is carving something out of a block of wood knows whether the knife goes deep or is just on the surface. Observing the breath like that, the mind becomes one-pointed and realizes meditative concentration. The boundless virtue of meditative concentration that takes us to the other shore is realized by the one-pointed mind of the bodhisattva in this way.

1 Elements of Meditation

WHOLESOME ELEMENTS

IN THE FIRST PASSAGE of "The Way of Realizing Meditation" Tang Hôi tells us that the virtue of meditative concentration is "making our mind upright again." He goes on to say that we can use wholesome mental formations to eliminate impurities.

> What is the boundless virtue of meditative concentration that can take us to the other shore? It is making our mind upright again. We devote our mind to one object and accumulate all the wholesome formations. We use thFese wholesome mental formations to eliminate the impurities that are still clinging to our mind. That is the boundless virtue of meditation that takes us to the other shore.

The five wholesome elements referred to here are initial thought, subsequent discursive thought, joy, happiness, and one-pointed mind. The first two wholesome elements that Tang Hôi mentions are the two aspects of right thinking. According to Buddhist psychology *(abhidharma),* thinking has two aspects, "initial thinking" *(vitarka)* and "subsequent discursive thought" *(vicara).* We can use "thinking" at the beginning of our meditation if it is right thinking. We do this by directing our mind towards an object and contemplating that object with the intention of understanding it. "Initial thinking," also known as "mental attention" *(manaskara),* means to give our attention to an object and stay with that object. Initial thinking is often likened to a butterfly that alights on a flower and gives its attention to it. "Subse-

43

quent discursive thought" is giving attention to the details of the object and is compared to a butterfly that makes deeper contact with the flower and flies around it. In the same way, in subsequent discursive thought, we contemplate more deeply the object that we have chosen for our meditation. Subsequent discursive thought is also called "investigation of phenomena" *(dharmapravicaya)* and is the second of the Seven Factors of Awakening.[1]

For example, when we breathe in and become aware of our in-breath, we give our attention to our in-breath—it becomes the object that we want to understand. In this instance, initial thinking is giving our attention to the in-breath and recognizing that it is an in-breath. Subsequent discursive thought is wanting to understand more about the in-breath. "What are the reasons for the in-breath being here? Is the in-breath born of itself? Without this element or that element how could there be breath? If the in-breath is born then certainly it has to die. But when it dies where does it go?" All these questions belong to the part of thinking that investigates a phenomenon in order to understand its nature deeply. So "right initial thinking" and "right subsequent discursive thought" are the first two wholesome elements.

The third and fourth wholesome elements referred to in Tang Hôi's essay are joy and happiness. In the *Anapananusmriti Sutra*[2] we are instructed to practice: *"Breathing in, I feel joy."* There are many simple things that can make us joyful. The fact that we are able to practice sitting meditation gives us joy because we know that there are many people who do not have the time to practice. The fact that we have the opportunity to practice meditation for ourselves, for our parents, grandparents, and children is a condition for joy. The fact that we have the opportunity to practice with a Sangha, that we can

---

1 The Seven Factors of Awakening are mindfulness, investigation of phenomena, diligence, joy, ease, concentration, and letting go. See Thich Nhat Hanh, *The Heart of the Buddha's Teaching*, chap. 26.

2 The *Sutra on the Full Awareness of Breathing*. See Thich Nhat Hanh, *Breathe! You Are Alive: Sutra on the Full Awareness of Breathing*, Revised Edition (Berkeley, CA: Parallax Press, 1996).

breathe in and out easily, and that we have good health are a few of many reasons to be happy.

As practitioners we should know how to produce the element called joy. We shouldn't think that when we practice meditation we have to give up happiness. Joy and happiness are essential wholesome elements of our meditation practice. If we practice sitting meditation or walking meditation without joy and happiness, our practice will not be beneficial.

Traditionally in Buddhism it is said that the principal reason for feeling joy is "distancing." Distancing means to move away from something and to relinquish it. For example, if we live in a city where we breathe in gas fumes and dust and hear the roar of traffic every day, we experience happiness when we leave the city and go to the country. There is a remarkable sense of well-being and joy in our heart when we can see the blue sky, the white clouds, and the vast fields of wheat. In the same way, when we sit in meditation, we give up all our worldly needs and occupations and begin to feel our body and mind becoming lighter. It is from this ability to let go that our joy and happiness are born. Distancing and relinquishing give rise to joy and happiness.

The fifth wholesome element referred to is a one-pointed mind. If our mind is dispersed, we cannot realize the wholesome elements that are available in our consciousness. A one-pointed mind is essential. It means that our mind is concentrated on an object—it has stopped running and is calm, it is no longer dispersed and is able to look deeply into the object of meditation. As a result there is insight.

Unwholesome Elements

The "impurities" that Tang Hôi refers to in the first passage are the garbage of our mind. They are elements that bring about suffering. Impurities can be beneficial for our happiness and liberation, but first they need to be composted or transformed. "Internal formations,"

formations that are created as a result of our sense perceptions, and the "Five Hindrances" *(panca nivarana)* are kinds of impurities.

THE FIVE HINDRANCES

The impurities are the elements that make our mind dark and propel us along paths of darkness and suffering. First of all the impurities are defined as the Five Hindrances. The Five Hindrances are obstacles we face in our meditation practice.

The first hindrance is craving or desire. It is as if we are thirsty for something. We think, "If I could only have that, my thirst would be quenched." In fact, the more we have the thirstier we become. It is like eating salt when we are thirsty; we just become more thirsty.

The second hindrance is hatred and anger. When we hate or are angry, it is the same as when we crave something—our mind cannot be at peace and we lose our freedom.

The third hindrance is sleepiness. Too much sleep can be a significant obstacle to the practice of meditation, and we need to look deeply within ourselves in order to understand the reasons for excessive sleepiness.

The fourth hindrance is agitation and regret. Agitation is the energy in us that is always pushing us to do something. Whether we are sitting or standing, we never feel at peace. Regret eats at our heart. It takes all the joy out of our life so that we no longer have the freedom to practice. Sometimes, however, regret helps us to make changes in our lives that benefit us. In that case, it is a wholesome mental formation. But regret that oppresses us and does not allow us to practice is an unwholesome mental formation. Regret is one of the four indeterminate mental formations—it can be wholesome or unwholesome.

The fifth hindrance is doubt. When we have doubt in our mind, we lose our peace, joy, and freedom, and this prevents us from entering into meditative concentration.

MEDITATION IS ELIMINATION

What is the boundless virtue of meditative concentration that can take us to the other shore? It is making our mind upright again. We devote our mind to one object and accumulate all the wholesome formations. We use these wholesome mental formations to eliminate the impurities that are still clinging to our mind. That is the boundless virtue of meditation that takes us to the other shore.

There are four meditative concentrations. The practice of the first meditative concentration is to eliminate craving and the going awry that are brought about by the five kinds of clinging. This clinging takes place when the eyes are in contact with form, the ears are in contact with sound, the nose is in contact with scent, the tongue with taste, the body with pleasant touch, and the mind gives rise to desire.

Craving here is an internal formation based on a pleasant feeling. When internal formations are rooted in pleasant feelings, we lose our freedom because we are always being forced to find ways of satisfying our craving. For example, suppose that you are persuaded by a friend to smoke cigarettes or use drugs. Once you are caught in the cycle of smoking or taking drugs, you have an internal formation. That internal formation is an attachment to a kind of pleasure.

Falling in love can also be an internal formation. When we fall in love with someone and cannot feel at peace, and we are always thinking of the object of our love and trying to find ways of coming close to it, we call this state of mind an internal formation or an internal knot. That internal knot has the capacity to order us to go in a certain direction. We do not know why we are going in that direction, but we cannot stop ourselves because the internal formation has a great deal of power over us.

A folk song of north Vietnam says: "You miss that person like you miss tobacco. You have buried your pipe, but then you go and dig it up again." We have decided that we are not going to smoke anymore. We have dug a hole in the earth and buried our pipe. But a few days later we cannot bear it anymore. We miss the tobacco so much that we have to go to the place where the pipe is buried and dig it up because we have an internal formation or an internal knot telling us to smoke.

When a young man has fallen in love with a girl, without knowing why, whenever he goes to the university, instead of taking the shortest route, he follows a very long way around because the girl's house is on that road. Although he has very little hope of seeing her when he passes, he still goes on that road in rain or shine. He does this because there is a force that is controlling him—this is called an internal knot. When he has an internal knot in his heart like this, he is not able to study or to practice because he is pulled after the object of his love and his mind cannot stay with the practice or his studies.

Tang Hôi tells us that when the nose smells a scent that is sweet and pleasant, the mind gives rise to desire. A scent, such as perfume, is something very light that you cannot catch or hold. It does not even weigh a gram, but it is powerful enough to form an internal knot within us.

The term "impurities" which Tang Hôi uses in the first sentence refers to internal formations or internal knots that are created as a result of sense perceptions. The impurities also include the Five Hindrances, which are obstacles in the practice of meditation. Tang Hôi refers to them as "going awry" or "leaning over to one side." This is the opposite of being upright and straight. Therefore, the Five Hindrances need to be eliminated.

When wholesome states of mind have come together, they are able to do the work called "eliminating" or "burning up" impurities —the afflictions, habit energies, and internal formations—in our minds. It is like putting a lens under the sun. If some dust were placed at the point where the light is concentrated, it would burst into flame. The same is true with meditation. If we use our one-pointed mind along with the other wholesome mental elements, we will be able to burn up and eliminate these impurities. We call this fire-like energy "concentration" or *samadhi*. That is what the ancestral teachers meant when they used the word "elimination."

2 The Four Meditative Concentrations

THE FIRST MEDITATIVE CONCENTRATION

In "The Way of Realizing Meditation,"
Tang Hôi states:

> The practice of the first meditative concentration is to eliminate craving and the going awry that are brought about by the five kinds of clinging.... Those who intend to realize the path at the very least should distance themselves from the sense desires.

We are able to realize the first meditative concentration when we have given up the objects of craving. This does not mean we understand the true nature of the objects of craving. At this point, we are aware that they have caused us to suffer and we know that we should keep away from them. Therefore, the first meditative concentration can be summarized as "letting go." If we want to be safe, we have to let go of the objects of desire.

Once we are aware of the suffering and the bondage brought about by the five kinds of clinging and are able to let go of the objects we crave, we can already begin to feel the peace of the first meditative concentration. A feeling of joy and happiness is born.

> When the whole mind, including the conscious mind and the unconscious store consciousness, has been cleared of all impurities, it is very bright. It is able to see the truth, and it reaches a state where there is nothing it does not understand. At that point the gods, the nagas, and the spirits are no longer able to

deceive the practitioner. Someone who realizes the first meditative concentration is like a person who has managed to escape from ten different enemies. She is alone on a high mountain, and, since no one knows where she is, she no longer has any reason to be afraid.

Although we have concentration at this stage, it is still weak. And although there is joy and happiness, they are not yet solid. Tang Hôi says this is like someone who has managed to distance herself from her enemies who are chasing her and trying to kill her. When she is able to escape from her enemies by climbing to the top of a high mountain, she feels more secure. However, what if they find her there? There is still fear in her mind. In reality, the greatest danger is not that these enemies will find her, but that she will go looking for them.

When someone is able to leave behind the sense desires, she feels pure and clear within, and her mind is at rest. When the first meditative concentration has been realized, the practitioner takes another step in the direction of the second meditative concentration.

THE SECOND MEDITATIVE CONCENTRATION

Our ability to distance ourselves in the first meditative concentration gives us happiness and peace of mind, but these two qualities are not yet very solid because they depend only on distancing. In the second meditative concentration the two kinds of thought, initial and discursive thinking, begin to disappear, and the one-pointed mind becomes more stable. When this happens, there is greater concentration and joy and happiness become deeper.

Someone who realizes the second meditative concentration is like a person who has managed to escape from his enemies.

Although he has gone deep into the mountains, he still has a little anxiety that those enemies could come and find him. So he wants to go deeper into the mountains to hide himself. Although the practitioner has left behind the five kinds of sensual desire and the Five Hindrances, he is still afraid that those enemies will come and find him and destroy his aspiration to be awakened.

We only need to hear some sentimental music for old seeds of attachment to come back to life. There is always the danger that we will step back into the world of sensuality and be caught once again in the bondage of the world. We no longer believe that these enemies are outside of us. We know that they come from within us, and we are right to fear them. When faced by these enemies, we may not have enough strength to protect ourselves on our own. That is why taking refuge in a Sangha, a community of practitioners, can be very helpful.

THE THIRD MEDITATIVE CONCENTRATION

When we realize the second meditative concentration, we leave all craving far behind, and it is no longer able to corrupt us. In the first meditative concentration, the wholesome mental formations and the unwholesome mental formations still oppose each other. The practitioner uses the wholesome mental formations to destroy the unwholesome ones, and, as the unwholesome ones retreat, the wholesome mental formations advance. In the second meditative concentration, the bliss of the first meditative concentration comes to an end. The practitioner no longer uses the method of destroying unwholesome mental formations by means of wholesome mental formations, and therefore the two elements of bliss and attachment to wholesomeness are no longer there. The ten unwholesome mental formations have come to an end and cease to manifest.

There is nothing that could make them invade the practitioner's mind from the outside anymore. It is like a spring of water on a high mountain peak. The clear water in the bed of the spring does not come from streams that run into the spring from outside, nor is it brought in by the rain that the nagas cause to fall. This water comes from the heart of the spring. Just as the clear water fills the bed of the spring, so the wholesome mental formations flow out from within the practitioner's mind, and unwholesome mental formations are not produced by sense objects that enter the practitioner by way of the eyes, ears, nose, and tongue. The meditator who has restrained the mind in this way begins to go in the direction of the third meditative concentration.

In the first meditative concentration, we still think that our enemies are outside of us. When we come to the second meditative concentration, we realize that our enemies do not invade us through the six doors of eyes, ears, nose, tongue, body, and mind. We know that our enemies are the seeds of bondage that lie within our own minds. Thus we are no longer afraid of what is outside of us, and we concern ourselves with what lies within us. In doing this, the joy of the first meditative concentration is transformed into a joy that is more solid.

The third meditative concentration is described as the wonderful happiness of giving up joy. When we come to the third meditative concentration, we give up the kind of joy that contains elements of excitement. When the initial and subsequent discursive thought of Right Thinking and the excitement of joy have fallen silent, then our joy is truly solid and is called "the wonderful happiness." This happiness is called "dwelling happily in the present moment" or "the food of the holy ones."

At the stage of the third meditative concentration, although we are still in the *Saha* World (the world of change and suffering), we are happy. We have begun to experience a holy fruit. In the *Sukhavati Sutra* there is the expression "the profane and the holy living together."

This means that the holy and unholy live together in one world. The holy have managed to leave behind impurities and wrong desires, and are able to touch the wonderful aspects of life—they are happy right in the present moment. The unholy are those who continue to suffer incessantly because they think they can only find happiness by leaving behind their present environment. This is the attitude of someone who is running away.

THE FOURTH MEDITATIVE CONCENTRATION

In the third meditative concentration the practitioner is able to maintain right mindfulness very solidly. Ideas of wholesome and unwholesome are not able to agitate her. Her mind is as unmovable as Mount Sumeru. The wholesome mental formations are not produced outside the mind, and therefore the wholesome and the unwholesome are not able to invade the mind. The mind is like the stem and roots of a lotus flower lying on the bed of a lake. The bud of the lotus flower is still covered by the water and has not lifted itself above the surface. In the third meditative concentration the calm and clarity are like a lotus flower. All impurities have been eliminated, and the body and mind are at peace. When the mind has been mastered in such a way, the meditator begins to go in the direction of the fourth meditative concentration.

On reaching the fourth meditative concentration, the practitioner has wholly eliminated ideas of wholesome and unwholesome. The mind does not long for the wholesome and does not hold on to the unwholesome. The content of the mind is as bright and clear as lapis lazuli. It is like a princess who has bathed and rubbed herself with fragrant oils. All her clothes are new, and she is clean and fragrant. When the mind of the bodhisattva has become straight and upright after achieving the fourth meditative concentration, the impurities that make her mind unstable no longer have the power to hide her mind from her.

When we come to the fourth meditative concentration the concepts of happiness and suffering have been released and all that is left is the one-pointed mind. In the process of practicing meditation we need the help of certain elements at the beginning, but we gradually let go of them as we no longer need them.

When we study the four meditative concentrations, we should remember that they are like a frame in which we place a picture—what is important is the content of the four meditative concentrations. The true meaning of meditative concentration is to let go in order to have freedom, peace, and joy. This is what we learn from the Four Establishments of Mindfulness, the Noble Eightfold Path, and mindfulness of breathing. Tang Hôi tells us that when a practitioner is able to let go, the mind becomes clear.

In former times, the bhikshu, after taking the midday meal and bathing, went deep into the mountains and sat at the foot of a tree in meditation. He placed one hand on top of the other, inclined his head forward a little, established the silence of mindfulness, and with one-pointed mind stilled his thoughts, destroying the Five Hindrances from within his mind. Once the Five Hindrances are destroyed, the practitioner's mind becomes clear. The darkness retreats, and the light remains.

The idea of the original mind that is bright and wonderfully clear is an important principle in Buddhism. Later on this principle was the foundation for the teachings on the *Buddhata* (Buddha nature) and Tathagatagarbha[1] (Tathagata[2] store). We can see this principle already present in Tang Hôi's teachings.

1 The later Mahayana sutras such as the *No-Increase No-Decrease*, the *Mahaparinirvana*, *The Lion's Roar of Queen Srimala*, and the *Lankavatara* all speak of Tathagatagarbha. In the *Lankavatara Sutra* a concentration called "Tathagatagarbha concentration" is taught.
2 Tathagata is another word for Buddha. It means "the one who comes and goes like that."

Tang Hôi gives five examples of the joy experienced by the practitioner when he is released from the Five Hindrances and the clear mind is revealed. In the first image, Tang Hôi compares leaving behind the Five Hindrances to a person that has been freed from the debt she owed. He says:

When we are able to destroy the Five Hindrances, then the wholesome dharmas will prosper and increase. It is like when a poor person has been able to pay off all her old debts and begins to make a profit, so that every day she has a little more than she had the day before. She feels very happy.

This is a useful metaphor. As long as someone craves for or is attached to something, such as anger, blaming, jealousy, or suspicion, then that person is in debt. Once we no longer have any debt weighing on us, we become a free person. We should ask ourselves whether we are still in debt and what wholesome mental formations we can develop to help us transform.

The second example is that of "a slave who has been given his freedom and the rights of citizenship." In former times, both in the East and in the West, there were systems of slavery. Many people were so poor that they had to sell their children as slaves to rich families. That child would have to work for twenty or thirty years in order to pay off the debt that his or her parents owed. When slaves were given their freedom, they were very happy. We can be happy like this when we give up our craving, anger, and doubt.

The third example is "when someone who has been seriously ill is healed." When someone in your family is very ill and bedridden for months or years, you cannot be happy. If you find a good doctor who is able to cure that person, then the whole family will be very happy.

The fourth example is "when someone who has committed a serious crime and been imprisoned is granted a reprieve and recovers his freedom."

The final example is "when someone crosses the ocean with a

cargo of precious jewels and, having passed through many difficulties, returns home to his family and feels tremendous joy." In all these examples Tang Hôi extols the joy we will feel when the Five Hindrances are eliminated.

When the mind continues to hold on to the Five Hindrances, we suffer like these five people before they were liberated. A bhikshu who sees the truth and eliminates the Five Hindrances is like the ordinary person when she is able to be liberated from the five misfortunes recounted above. When the hindrances are made to retreat, then the light of the mind shines out. All the unwholesome mental formations are destroyed.

3 The Arhat Is the Bodhisattva

L ET'S TURN to a comparison of the *Sutra of Forty-Two Chapters*[1] and Tang Hôi's writings. The *Sutra of Forty-Two Chapters* talks about the fruit of arhatship and the deep influence of an arhat's life on his surroundings. It states:

> *The life span of an arhat is everlasting. It cannot be measured in terms of years and months. Earth and sky everywhere are shaken [when the fruit of arhatship is realized].*

The following extract from Tang Hôi's essay "The Way of Realizing Meditation" is similar to what is said about the arhat in the *Sutra of Forty-Two Chapters*:

> Just as a painter has the freedom to use whatever colors and forms she likes, or a potter can produce whatever vessels he likes out of clay, or a goldsmith according to his wishes can produce

---

1 According to tradition, the *Sutra of Forty-Two Chapters* first appeared in the Luoyang center after King Han Mingdi sent a delegation to India to retrieve it. However, Master Dao An, the author of the index to the earlier Chinese Canon, did not mention the *Sutra of Forty-Two Chapters,* nor did he include *Dispelling Doubts* of Mouzi. The reason for this is that he was from further north and he only knew about the sutras which were obtainable there. Although the *Sutra of Forty-Two Chapters* was not available in the northern Luoyang center, it was available in the Luy Lau and the Peng Cheng centers. The historical records tell us that the *Sutra of Forty-Two Chapters* was known in the Peng Cheng center. At the same time *Dispelling Doubts,* which was written in the second century, mentions the *Sutra of Forty-Two Chapters,* which means that it must have appeared in the Luy Lau center where Mouzi received his Buddhist studies.

hundreds or thousands of different forms of skillfully made adornments, the bodhisattva who makes her mind calm and clear and realizes the fourth meditative concentration can do whatever she likes. She can fly or walk in space, travel under the water, appear in many bodies in different places, move through matter without it being an obstruction, appear and disappear at will, touch the sun and the moon, cause the earth and sky to tremble, see through matter, and hear sounds from afar. There is nothing she does not see or hear.

The only difference between the *Sutra of Forty-Two Chapters* and Tang Hôi's essay is that these qualities are said to belong to the arhat in the former, while Tang Hôi says that they belong to the bodhisattva in the latter. Tang Hôi uses the term "bodhisattva" because he was trained in the Mahayana tradition.

When his mind is concentrated and his observation is clear, the bodhisattva understands all things. He understands the state of things before the heavens, the earth, and living beings existed. He can know the minds of living beings in the ten directions in the present moment. He can know what has happened to them from when they were first conceived. He can see the cycle of birth and death of living beings: how they are born as humans or gods, and how they fall into the hell realms, the hungry ghost realms, and the animal realms. He sees how they undergo retribution for their wrongdoing when they have exhausted the merit of their virtuous actions, and how, when their misfortune has come to an end, they can again enjoy happiness. In short, nothing can happen near or far away that the bodhisattva does not know about. That is the effect of the fourth meditative concentration.

In the following extract Tang Hôi talks about the important place of the fourth meditative concentration, saying that without it the practitioner will not be able to reach the fruits of practice such as the six or the five higher knowledges *(abhijña)*[2] and the fruit of Buddhahood. From the following quotation, we can see the influence of sutras that give a high value to the four meditative concentrations:

Someone who wants to realize the fruits of stream-enterer, once-returner, no-returner, and arhatship or the highest right awakening that is the wisdom of equalness of the Awakened One, has to realize the fourth meditative concentration. Once this has been attained, anything is possible. Just as all the animal, plant, and mineral species come from the earth, so the fruits of the practice, such as the five higher knowledges to the state of Tathagata, all come from success in the practice of the fourth meditative concentration. When people build, the earth is the place where they lay the foundations. So the fourth meditative concentration is the foundation for realization in the practice. The World-Honored One has taught: "Living beings, including the gods and the holy ones, however high their intelligence and wonderful their skills may be, if they do not practice what is written in the sutras, and they do not realize the concentration[3] that eliminates the unwholesome states of mind, must still be ranked among those who are in a dream."

When reading this we should remember that the ancestral teachers included the four meditative concentrations as an essential part of the Buddhist practice very early in the history of Buddhism, maybe a hundred years after the Buddha's *parinirvana*[4] in 485 B.C.E. There is a great deal of evidence that the four meditative concentrations were

2 The abhijñas are: 1) the ability to move through solid objects, 2) divine hearing, 3) knowledge of the thoughts of others, 4) recollection of one's previous lives, and 5) knowledge of the previous lives of other beings. Sometimes a sixth is added — the assurance of final liberation through the knowledge of one's impurities.

3 Concentration here means gradually giving up and eliminating psychological elements that are not necessary.

4 This is the way in which the Buddha left this life. It is a state of complete liberation.

not taught by the Buddha himself, although he had practiced them. In the *Anapanasati Sutta* in Pali there is absolutely no mention of the four meditative concentrations. However, in the *Anapananusmriti* chapter of the Chinese Canon *(Samyukta Agama),* the four meditative concentrations are mentioned. This inconsistency occurs frequently in the two canons, and usually such an inconsistency indicates that there has been a later addition, in this case the addition of the four meditative concentrations.

The Tamrasatiya school and the Sarvastivada school were separated from each other several hundred years before the Christian Era. The Sarvastivada school went to the northwest of India and lasted for more than a thousand years, and the Tamrasatiya school went south to Sri Lanka. It is very fortunate that today two canons of the Buddha's teachings — the canons of the Sarvastivada school and the Tamrasatiya school — still exist and can be compared. The canon of the Sarvastivada school is extant in Chinese, and that of the Tamrasatiya school is extant in Pali.

In comparing the sutras from these two canons, when there is text that is identical in both sutras, we know that this text must have existed before the separation. When there is text found in the sutras of one canon but not in the sutras of the other canon, it is possible that later additions were made. Based on comparative studies of this kind, we know that the principles of the four meditative concentrations were introduced into the Buddha's teachings quite soon after he passed away. Later these principles were gradually introduced into sutras in which they had not been mentioned earlier. The four meditative concentrations were added to both the Chinese Canon and the Pali Canon in this way.

As mentioned earlier, the four meditative concentrations are to be viewed as a guide. The true meaning or content of meditative concentration is what is important — letting go in order to have freedom, peace, and joy. Tang Hôi asks the question whether the practice of the fourth meditative concentration is sufficient for the realization of the fruit of arhatship — liberation. The answer is: It could be, but it is not necessarily so. It is possible that the practitioner experiences considerable bliss and tranquility during the fourth meditative concentration, but if the content of the meditation is poor in terms of insight and compassion, the practice will not give rise to arhatship — the practitioner may be born in the realm of the gods, but he will not be able to realize the fruit of liberation. Tang Hôi states:

> If the mind is still at the first meditative concentration, then it is not yet possible to realize the fruit of arhatship, and when the practitioner passes away she will be reborn in the seventh heaven and will dwell there for one lifetime. If the practitioner has realized the second meditative concentration, when she passes away she will be born in the eleventh heaven and will pass two lifetimes there. If the mind of the practitioner is established in the third meditative concentration, she will be born in the fifteenth heaven and will pass three lifetimes there. If her mind is established in the fourth meditative concentration, she will be born in the nineteenth heaven and will pass sixteen lifetimes there.

To be born in the realms of the gods is not liberation; it is not the aim of the practice. This is not why the Buddha practiced. The Buddha practiced in order to be liberated. Therefore these lines of Tang Hôi show that the fourth meditative concentration is not something absolutely necessary for the practice of Buddhism. The fourth meditative concentration is only a frame for our practice. The essence of the practice is mindfulness of breathing, the Four Establishments of Mindfulness, the Eight Recollections, and the Ten Contemplations because these exercises help us to look deeply so that we can realize understanding and love.

4 The Path and
the Aspiration to Be Awakened

AT THE BEGINNING of the third century C.E., a systematic way of translating technical Buddhist terminology from Sanskrit into Chinese had not been established. The sutras of the *Agamas*[1] were first translated in the fourth and fifth centuries C.E. from Sanskrit. During his time, Tang Hôi found suitable Chinese expressions for Sanskrit Buddhist terms, but these expressions were not always used in later times. For example, the words *anatma* (nonself), *bhagavan* (World-Honored Lord), and sramana (monk) were all translated differently by Tang Hôi than they were by later translators.

When monks started translating sutras from Sanskrit into Chinese, many Taoist expressions were used to convey Buddhist ideas. For example, the expression *wu wei*, which means "non-action," was used by the Buddhists of that time to translate the Sanskrit word *asamskrita,* meaning "the uncompounded." Properly the word *tao* is used to translate the Sanskrit word *marga* ("path"). Here, however, *tao* is used to translate *bodhi* ("awakening"). In this case to achieve *tao* means to realize awakening. Similarly, when the word *tao* is followed by the word *tam* ("mind"), it does not mean "the mind of the path," it means "the bodhi mind" *(bodhicitta).*[2]

Tang Hôi repeats a certain expression many times in "The Way of Realizing Meditation." It has been translated here as "the aspiration to

1 The collection of discourses given by the Buddha that were written down in Sanskrit. The *Agamas* were translated into Chinese and can now be found in the Chinese Canon, although they are no longer extant in Sanskrit. The collections in Pali are given the name *Nikaya.*
2 In the poem "Song of Realizing the Way" written by Meditation Master Xuan Jiao, the word "way" also has the meaning of awakening.

be awakened." When Tang Hôi uses the expression "aspiration to be awakened," it is equivalent to the expression "Beginner's Mind." It is an intention to realize the path, to be awakened, to practice, and to be successful in the practice so that the fruit of our practice can help others. It is the aspiration to share happiness with others, and that is called "bodhicitta," or here, "the aspiration to be awakened."

In our daily lives, we need to know how to nourish our aspiration to be awakened, or this aspiration will slowly wither and fade. This would be a tremendous loss. By practicing in a Sangha, we can nourish our aspiration to be awakened and help it to grow stronger every day.

5 Nourishing the Aspiration to Be Awakened

I n *The Collection on the Six Paramitas,* Tang Hôi brings together many stories from the life and former lives of the Buddha. He uses several hundred of these stories in order to clarify our understanding of the Six Paramitas. In connection with the practice of meditative concentration, Tang Hôi tells the story of Prince Siddhartha leaving the palace four times in order to meet people outside of the palace. On one of these excursions Siddhartha met a very old person. The image of that old person struck his heart so deeply that he could not eat or sleep. That image nourished his aspiration to be awakened, and he practiced in order to overcome old age, sickness, and death.

Siddhartha had his very first experience of suffering when he was nine years old. At that time, he observed a farmer ploughing a rice field. As the blade of the plough turned the earth over, it cut the worms in two. Small birds flew down, picked up the worms in their beaks, and ate them. Larger birds chased after the small birds and pecked at them. It was the first time he had seen such scenes, and they left a very deep impression on him. Siddhartha had discovered the suffering that until then had been hidden from him. At the sight of this suffering, he lost his peace of mind and, even as a young child, he was moved to sit still and contemplate. The sun was blazing in the sky, so, finding the shade of a rose-apple tree, he sat cross-legged and allowed his mind to penetrate the images he had just seen. That was the first time Siddhartha practiced sitting meditation. He practiced without knowing he was practicing.

King Suddhodana and Queen Mahagotami went looking for him and found him sitting at the foot of a tree on the hill. He looked so beautiful that the queen wept. However, the king was very worried that his son might decide to become a monk. This, he thought, would be a great misfortune for his family. A group of young children were playing and laughing nearby, and Queen Mahagotami said to them: "Children, don't make any noise. Don't you see the prince sitting in meditation? Allow him to sit longer."[1]

Tang Hôi teaches that when we practice awakening, we need to have right mindfulness in order to look deeply into the things that we see or hear. We should be in touch in such a way that our aspiration to be awakened grows firmer every day. We should not be like a branch of duckweed bobbing up and down on the water, allowing itself to be pulled in any direction. We need strong determination, and that is called the aspiration to be awakened.

Tang Hôi comments on the many opportunities available to nourish our aspiration:

> There are many circumstances that are favorable to the bodhisattva's aspiration to be awakened and help her to achieve the state of inner silence and one-pointed mind, which makes it possible to have meditative concentration. For example, when bodhisattvas see an old person with white hair, loose teeth, and a body in a process of deterioration, they wake themselves up by remembering that their own body will be like that in the future. Because of that, they realize meditative concentration.

The following passage from "The Way of Realizing Meditation" is a repetition of what is found in the *Satipatthana*[2] and *Kayagata-sati*[3] *Suttas:*

1 For more on the life of the Buddha, see Thich Nhat Hanh, *Old Path White Clouds: Walking in the Footsteps of the Buddha* (Berkeley, CA: Parallax Press, 1991).
2 *Majjhima Nikaya,* Sutta No. 10.
3 *Majjhima Nikaya,* Sutta No. 119.

When bodhisattvas see someone who is sick, afflicted in body and mind, their life at risk, and pain like a knife cutting into the flesh, they suffer and wake themselves up by thinking that their own body in time will be like that, and thus they realize meditative concentration.

Here "meditative concentration" means the force of mindfulness and the force of concentration. What we see moves us to act, and our action is looking deeply.

The bodhisattvas see living beings die. The breath stops, the body grows cold, the consciousness leaves the body, the corpse grows rigid, and all loved ones are left behind. The corpse is taken out to a deserted place, and a couple of days later it becomes fetid. Hyenas and vultures come and eat it, insects and maggots are born inside it and consume it. Blood and a foul-smelling substance trickle out of the corpse onto the earth, and then the bones are scattered in different places. A leg bone is in one place, an arm bone in another, the skull and the teeth are somewhere else. Someone who practices awakening meditates that for as long as there is birth there is death; the life of a human being, like everything else, is like a magic display. When something is composed of different elements, it will decompose. When consciousness leaves the body, it decomposes. We cannot avoid death, and our very own body will also come to this state of decomposition.

It takes a person like Siddhartha to be able to look deeply when he sees a corpse. Even though Siddhartha lived in a palace where there was good food and music, and where he had a wife and a beautiful child, these things did not keep him from remembering the corpse he had seen on the road, nor did it stop his deep aspiration to study and practice in order to discover a path that would take him and the people he loved beyond suffering.

A person who does not practice might say when encountering a corpse, "Oh, he's dead. At least it wasn't me. There is still a long time to go before I die." It is as if we are sitting on a bomb that is about to go off, but we feel perfectly secure.

> Seeing this, the bodhisattva feels compassion and makes her mind one-pointed in order to realize meditative concentration. The bodhisattva may see a corpse that has been lying for a long time, the bones have rotted and become dust and earth, and she contemplates deeply, telling herself: "My own body is like that." For that reason she realizes meditative concentration.

Tang Hôi speaks of the bodhisattva's compassion for those who are suffering:

> The bodhisattva hears about the fierce suffering of the blazing fires and boiling water in the hell realms, the long-lasting hunger and thirst of the hungry ghosts, and the pain of the animals who are slaughtered and cut into pieces to be food for human beings. Contemplating like this, the bodhisattva is startled and makes his mind one-pointed in order to realize meditative concentration.

When we see people selling pieces of red flesh, we do not see the things that Siddhartha saw. We do not see an animal in the prime of life having its neck broken and being cut into pieces. Because we lack awareness, we do not see the suffering of living beings.

Here we see once more the expression "aspiration to be awakened":

> The bodhisattva sees a poor person dying of hunger or cold, or he sees a criminal sentenced to death by the king, and he meditates: "That person has fallen into misfortune because he does not practice the aspiration to be awakened. If I do not practice diligently I could also find myself in such a situation."

Contemplating like that he makes his mind one-pointed in order to realize meditative concentration.

Here the bodhisattva meditates on war, starvation, and social injustice:

The bodhisattva sees a year when the crops fail, the poor people are starving, and they rise up in revolt. This causes a war, and everywhere there are corpses. At this he feels compassion and thinks that if he did not practice to be awakened, he too would behave like that, and so he makes his mind one-pointed in order to realize meditative concentration.

THE FIVE MEDITATIONS ON CHANGE

In "The Way of Realizing Meditative Concentration," Tang Hôi also teaches the five ways of looking deeply or five ways of meditation.

The bodhisattva uses the five methods of meditating on the body. First, he meditates on the changes of the face. Second, he meditates on the changes between suffering and happiness. Third, he meditates on the changes of intention. Fourth, he meditates on the changes in the body. Fifth, he meditates on the changes between wholesome and unwholesome. These changes take place like a stream of flowing water, always following one after the other. Meditating like this, he makes his mind one-pointed in order to realize meditative concentration.

The first meditation is on the changes of the face. Tang Hôi teaches us to look deeply at our face in a mirror. Our face is a bell of mindfulness. The sutras often give the example of a person who has just bathed, has put on clean clothes, and looks into a mirror or into a clear bowl of water. If he sees that his face is clean and there is not any mark left on it, then he is happy. He says: "My face is clean enough." A person who has unwholesome energies and internal formations knows that his face is not yet very clean and there are still marks of dirt on it. When he knows about those dirty marks, he has to do something to wipe them clean. This practice is called "looking in the mirror."[4]

Tang Hôi says that we should frequently look deeply at faces, the faces of others and our own faces. We know that faces do not stay the same, they are always changing. If the face of someone we know is sad, we should remind ourselves that her face will not always be like that. We or even she herself could help that face to change by a smile, by the light in our eyes, or by some action. It is the same for us when we are not happy. If we know how to breathe, how to practice walking meditation, and how to nourish ourselves with feelings of joy, then our faces will change too.

The second meditation is on the change of suffering and joy. We are suffering now, but soon we could be happy. We should not think that we will continue to suffer all our lives. This is the same for other people. We should not think that a person who is suffering will never feel joyful. If she knows how to practice, if she has a Sangha, if we help her, then she will be able to change her suffering into happiness. If we live without mindfulness and a daily practice, today's happiness will also disappear. Therefore, when we look into the changing nature of suffering and happiness, we know that we have to practice.

The third meditation is on the change of intention. Today we want this, but tomorrow we want something different. Today we think that this is a necessary condition for happiness, then we stumble and fall and see that it is not happiness. From this meditation on change of intention, we see our changing intentions and we can learn to make intentions that will benefit ourselves and others.

The fourth meditation is the meditation on the change of the

4 This example is found in the *Anumana Sutta, Majjhima Nikaya,* Sutta No. 15.

body. A person who is in good health can fall sick. A person who is young will grow old. A person who is ill can become well. Generally we think that the other person will always be the way we picture her, but in fact she changes every day, in body and in mind. Thanks to that change, we have the opportunity to transform.

For meditation on impermanence of the body, we can observe that although today we are still young, there will be a time when we will grow old. Today our legs are strong and we are able to run, but in time we may not be able to move quickly. In this way, meditating on change in our body helps us to see more deeply into the nature of life.

The fifth meditation is on the change of the wholesome and the unwholesome. The wholesome is able to turn into the unwholesome and the unwholesome can change into the wholesome. The beautiful can change into the ugly, and the ugly can change into the beautiful. Wholesome and unwholesome are both impermanent. Therefore, when we see the wholesome in our own minds or in the mind of another, we know that if we do not nourish that wholesome element, it could become something unwholesome in the future. If we know how to meditate, we can see the afflictions in our minds and transform them into peace, joy, and happiness. In Buddhism there is the expression, "the afflictions are awakening." It means that flowers can be fertilized with garbage. Without the garbage, there cannot be flowers.

THE CONTEMPLATIONS

It is clear from his works that at the beginning of the third century Tang Hôi was teaching mindfulness of breathing *(anapananusmriti)* and the Four Establishments of Mindfulness. Mindfulness of breathing was the basis of the practice that he taught. A natural result of the practice of mindful breathing is the practice of mindfulness of the body in the body, the feelings in the feelings, mental formations in the mental formations, and objects of mind in objects of mind. So mindfulness of breathing is practiced together with the Four Establishments of Mindfulness.[5]

He was also teaching the practice of the Eight Recollections—the recollections of Buddha, Dharma, Sangha, the Mindfulness Trainings, Equanimity, the God Realms, Breathing, and Death. "Recollection" *(anusmriti)* is also translated as "mindfulness." This implies that in the third century C.E., the people in Vietnam practiced meditation using the Eight Recollections.

Tang Hôi also taught the practice of contemplation *(samjña).* He taught the Ten Contemplations, which are the Contemplations on Impermanence, Suffering, Nonself, Food, the Impossibility of Finding Happiness in Any Worldly Thing, Death, Many Wrongdoings, Giving Up, Cutting Off, and Ending.

CONTEMPLATION ON FOOD

> When food goes into the mouth it seems to be fragrant and appetizing. But afterwards it is mixed with saliva and the digestive juices in the stomach and intestine, and finally it turns into excrement. Recollecting this, the bodhisattva is startled and makes her mind one-pointed in order to realize meditative concentration.

When we contemplate the food that we see on our plate, it looks very attractive and appetizing. But once it is in our mouth, it mixes with our saliva as we chew it. When it reaches the stomach and mixes with the sour, digestive juices, it is no longer attractive. That is what is meant by the Contemplation on Food. In the Five Contemplations,[6] which

---

5 See Thich Nhat Hanh, *Transformation & Healing: Sutra on the Four Establishments of Mindfulness* (Berkeley, CA: Parallax Press, 1990).
6 See Thich Nhat Hanh, *Plum Village Chanting and Recitation Book* (Berkeley, CA: Parallax Press, 2000).

we read before we begin to eat, one of the contemplations mentions greed: "May we transform our unskillful states of mind, and learn to eat with moderation." The Contemplation on Food helps us to do this.

CONTEMPLATION ON THE IMPOSSIBILITY OF FINDING HAPPINESS IN ANY WORLDLY THING

The Contemplation on the Impossibility of Finding Happiness in Any Worldly Thing helps us look carefully at the things in the world that are said to bring happiness. For example, to sit glued to the television every day for four hours is not real happiness. To stay up all night dancing or frequenting places where alcohol is consumed is considered to be pleasurable, but we know that too much of this kind of activity is not good for our health. An awakened person sees that what the world calls happiness brings about suffering, ill health, and a sense of meaninglessness. And when she sees that, she is no longer attracted to these things.

Three years ago a child came to Plum Village with his mother. Many parents think that however bad their children may be, if they bring them to Plum Village they will become as good as gold. When the child first arrived he was extremely bored. His mother had lured him to Plum Village with a promise to go to the sea. Looking at the program of daily activities, the child remarked: "It's like a prison here. They tell you that you have to do this now, and later you have to do that, and then later on you have to do something else. Why do you force me to stay here? It's like being in an army camp." The child also wanted to know if there was a television he could watch. When the novice monks replied "no," he said: "Then it's not possible for me to stay here." The child really thought that if there was no television he would die.

The mother did not want to leave, but did not know what to do. She went to one of the nuns to ask for help. The nun suggested that the mother persuade her son to stay for one day and if after that he still did not want to stay, she should take him to the sea. The child agreed to stay for twenty-four hours and began to play with the children who had practiced for many years in Plum Village. While he was playing with them, he experienced the wholesome joy of these children. Unconsciously he realized that even though there was no television, he could still survive.

When the twenty-four hours were up, his mother asked him: "Do you want to go to the sea now?" He replied: "I don't want to go, I want to stay here." Within twenty-four hours, thanks to the Sangha of children, the new child was able to discover something that he had never seen before: it is possible to live without a television. There were many joys other than watching television that were wholesome and able to nourish him, but he had not yet been in touch with them. When we discover true happiness we are able to let go of the false shadows of happiness, namely, the sensual pleasures. Sometimes we refer to false happiness as a plastic worm that is used as bait to catch fish. Thinking that the plastic worm will be tasty food, the fish puts it in his mouth and gets caught on the hook.

THE CONTEMPLATION ON DEATH

In addition to the Recollection on Death, Tang Hôi teaches the Contemplation on Death. These two practices are roughly equivalent. The Recollection on Death means that we remind ourselves of the reality of death. The Contemplation on Death means we look deeply into the nature of death. Tang Hôi describes how after death the body gradually grows cold and is bereft of life, and begins to ooze all sorts of unpleasant liquids. Contemplating death in this manner is called the Nine Contemplations, because we contemplate each of the nine stages in the dissolution of a corpse.

CONTEMPLATION ON THE MANY WRONGDOINGS

The Contemplation on the Many Wrongdoings is being able to see that even when we do not want to do something wrong or cruel, we do them anyway because our environment is bad or our habit energies are strong. Our environment and our habit energies are like a stream of water that pulls us along. Even when we are aware that a certain food we eat or beverage we drink, a television program we watch, or words we say will be harmful in some way and be the cause of attachment and guilt, our habit energy or our environment is stronger than we are. Like powerful river rapids, they pull us along and, in the end, we cannot stop ourselves.

Monks and nuns, determined to overcome those rapids of habit energy, enter an entirely different environment. In this new environment, a monastic is able to understand his habit energy in the light of his practice of mindfulness. She learns to recognize the process and the environment that force people to do, say, and think the things that they do not want to do, say, or think. Anyone who is able to live mindfully and cultivate a mind of awakening will in time be able to bring about conditions that will help others. When a person who has nearly died from drowning manages to get to the shore, she can build a boat in which she can rescue others who are about to drown. She builds this boat for her friends and relatives and for others as well.

CONTEMPLATION ON GIVING UP

The Contemplation on Giving Up means we give up and leave behind the environment of bondage — the deceptions and toxins that destroy our body and mind. It is possible that on our own we would not have the strength to leave these things behind. In the *Anapananusmriti Sutra* the Buddha taught us a practice of breathing that can help us in letting go. Belonging to a Sangha and having a daily practice will also enable us to do so.

CONTEMPLATION ON CUTTING OFF

The Contemplation on Cutting Off means to practice not allowing
things that harm us to continue. It requires that we know clearly the
true face of the object of our mind and that we can call it by its true
name. Then we will come to know what causes destruction to our
bodies and minds, and we will be determined to cut it off.

CONTEMPLATION ON ENDING

The Contemplation on Ending means ending all wrong perceptions
and the infatuations, hatred, and anger that are born as a result of these
wrong perceptions. This contemplation is also accompanied by mindful breathing and is taught by the Buddha in the *Sutra on the Full
Awareness of Breathing.*[7] Ideas such as birth and death, existence and
nonexistence, one and many, coming and going, have ended. Other
ideas such as nirvana, samsara, and happiness, and even ideas such as
impermanence, nonself, suffering, and emptiness are overcome and
ended. In short, all ideas need to be ended. The essence of nirvana is
to be able to go beyond words and perceptions. Here "ending" means
"ending all the wrong perceptions." Wrong perceptions are the basis
of craving, infatuation, hatred, jealousy, and fear. By putting an end to
these wrong perceptions, we put an end to the suffering and affliction
produced by them. Only then can real happiness arise.

   Tang Hôi also teaches us to look deeply at poverty, war, prosperity, impurity, and decline and to nourish our compassion and loving
kindness. These were all objects of meditation practice that he taught
in the beginning of the third century. Tang Hôi had read the early
chapters of the *Avatamsaka Sutra* (the *Dasabhumika* and the *Gand-
havyuha*) in Chinese. He had also read the *Lotus Sutra.* These sutras are
reflected in his writings which we are studying now.

---

7 See Thich Nhat Hanh, *Breathe! You Are Alive: Sutra on the Full Awareness of Breathing.*

THE RECOLLECTIONS

Tang Hôi uses the expression "mindfulness of the body." The Sanskrit word for "mindfulness" in this context is "anusmriti." First we practice mindfulness of our body, then we practice the Nine Contemplations on the decomposition of the body until it becomes ash or dust. Then we contemplate the suffering of poverty, war, and the slaughter of animals for food. We contemplate prosperity and decline. We contemplate impermanence and impurity. We contemplate the fact that riches cannot be maintained forever and neither can youth. After that we contemplate the Buddha. The following excerpts are on the recollection of Buddha, Dharma, and Sangha:

> When the bodhisattva contemplates the incomparably wonderful signs of the Buddha's body,[8] he knows that these signs are due to the purification of the practice over many lifetimes. For only then is a person able to tame the minds of living beings. Keeping this contemplation in his mind, great joy arises in him and, because of that, he makes his mind one-pointed in order to realize meditative concentration.
>
> The bodhisattva contemplates on the deep and wonderful teachings of the Dharma and on the high level of pure practice of the sramanas[9] and makes his mind one-pointed in order to realize meditative concentration.

This contemplation is called "the recollection of the gods." We can recollect the Buddha, the Dharma, the Sangha, the precepts, and the gods:

> He makes a deep aspiration to use his body to realize awakening and to build up his virtue now and in the future and

8 This means that we meditate on the thirty-two special aspects of the Buddha's body, which manifest the beauty of the Buddha's spirit.
9 Monks who have realized the practice.

makes his mind one-pointed in order to realize meditative concentration.

Contemplating the desires of an ignorant person and the behavior that runs counter to the true teachings, she sees that these things not only bring about toil and suffering but also lead to further wrongdoing. Contemplating how human beings are born in the world of the gods because they observe the precepts and practice vegetarianism and as gods are able to enjoy an extremely long life span and happiness, the bodhisattva makes her mind one-pointed in order to realize meditative concentration.

This meditation can also be called "recollection of the Dharma":

When the bodhisattva receives the teachings of the Buddha, studies and experiences them, and is taught and instructed by the noble Sangha, her mind rejoices and because of that she makes her mind one-pointed in order to realize meditative concentration.

This is the contemplation on the suffering of life:

Any of the species of living beings that come to be will pass away, and when there is passing away there is suffering. Contemplating like this, the bodhisattva gives rise to compassion and makes his mind one-pointed in order to realize meditative concentration.

This is a method of contemplation called "no worldly thing can bring happiness." It means that the practitioner is able to see that the things that the world calls happiness are not really happiness:

The nature of sentient beings is such that they cannot guarantee the survival of their own person. Every one of them has to go through processes of change. Someone who practices awakening has fear, knowing that when he passes away he could fall into paths of cruel suffering. Seeing that prosperity and honors, whether they are real or false, are all like a dream, the bodhisattva sees the importance of awakening and for that reason makes his mind one-pointed in order to realize meditative concentration.

THE PRACTICE OF KOAN

How should the bodhisattva use meditative concentration in the right way? For example, when his eyes observe a dead person from the head down to the feet, his mind should contemplate deeply and note exactly what he sees. He should maintain this image at all times—when he is walking, standing, lying down, sitting, eating, drinking, or doing any one of ten thousand other things. He should maintain this meditation in his heart in order to consolidate his aspiration to be awakened, and then he will be able to nourish the object of his mindfulness in meditative concentration naturally and easily. It is like when someone takes a little rice from a pot with chopsticks to see if it is cooked. He only needs to take one grain and observe it. If that grain is cooked, then the whole pot of rice is cooked. Once the aspiration to be awakened is strong, then the whole mind will follow its direction quite naturally, as water follows water in a stream.

The teaching given above is connected to what was later to become the practice of *koan*.[10] The meditation on koan is a method of instruction that helps a practitioner put his whole mind, thought,

10 Meditation on koan has held an important place in the history of Chinese Buddhist meditation. A koan is a proposition we look at deeply, and we nourish this meditation in us day and night.

and life into the practice. Whether he is walking, standing, sitting, or lying down, whether it is night or day, he continues to practice the koan.

This principle is in the teachings of Tang Hôi. According to him, there is a very simple way of practicing koan. When we know how to live our daily life in mindfulness, whatever we are in touch with becomes a koan. For example, if we hear the howl of a pig that is being slaughtered in the dead of night, this yell can become the object of our looking deeply. It is something we cannot forget. Whether we are walking, standing, lying down, or sitting, we hold on to that sound.

When a scientist is researching something, he is always attentive to the object of his research. When Newton was researching the principle of gravity, his mind was wholly attentive to that object—when walking, standing, lying down, or sitting he was wholly attentive to the object of his research. That is why when he was sitting under an apple tree and an apple fell onto his head he was able to formulate the law of gravity.

To practice being awakened, we need the same level of concentration. Whether walking, standing, lying down, or sitting, we should give our attention to the object of our looking deeply. Only then will our concentration become strong enough to break through the veil of ignorance in order to see the truth. So the practice of meditative concentration does not just mean sitting meditation. Whether we are eating a meal, drinking tea, or washing dishes, whatever we are doing, we can be practicing meditation. This is not different from practicing with a koan.

Here we see that Tang Hôi is an authentic patriarch of the Meditation school, not only for Vietnam, but also for China and Japan in time to come. "Once the aspiration to be awakened is strong, then the whole mind will follow its direction quite naturally, as water follows water in a stream." Water pushes water forward and quite naturally we go in that direction. We do not have to make laborious efforts; our mind is quite naturally concentrated. In order to be concentrated—to give all our mental power to the object of our observation—the secret is that we must be determined in our aspiration to be awakened. The "aspiration to be awakened" (bodhicitta, or Beginner's Mind) also means the practice of koan.

In the traditional practice of koan the student meets the meditation teacher and is told: "My child, you should look deeply and tell me: If everything goes back to the one, then where does the one go back to?" From the day the student receives this koan, she could stop eating and sleeping. Or when she is eating she could simply eat, and when she is sleeping she could simply sleep. The koan continues to be there in every moment. While she is sleeping, her unconscious mind continues to work with the koan.

If she just gives half her attention to the question, she will never resolve it. When her teacher gives the koan: "Please tell me: What was your face like before your grandmother was born?" or "Who is the one who recollects the Buddha?" the student has to invest her whole person into that question—body and mind—all day and all night long, embracing the koan in order to break it open and to give rise to the truth.

Tang Hôi says that when our aspiration to be awakened is strong, we do not need to force ourselves to concentrate or look deeply, we will quite naturally move in that direction. When we have a very deep desire, a great aspiration, we are like a scientist who wants to discover something very important. Our body and mind, as well as our daily life, all go in that direction.

PART II:

The Preface to the *Anapananusmriti Sutra*

IN THIS SECTION the full text of the Preface to the *Anapananusmriti Sutra* by Tang Hôi is presented, followed by the author's commentary. The preface was written by Tang Hôi prior to 229 C.E., before he left Jiaozhou for Dong Wu, and after he wrote "The Way of Realizing Meditation." We find a greater depth and clarity of Tang Hôi's expression of the Mahayana in this second work.

The Preface to the *Anapananusmriti Sutra*

BY TANG HÔI

Translated into Vietnamese by Thich Nhat Hanh and Chan Vien Quang
Translated into English by Sr. Annabel Laity

MINDFULNESS OF BREATHING is the great vehicle used by the Buddhas to save beings who are tossing up and down and drowning in the ocean of great suffering. There are six kinds of mindfulness of breathing aimed at treating the six senses. The six senses have an internal and an external aspect. The internal aspect of the six senses are the eyes, ears, nose, tongue, body, and mind. The external aspect of the six senses are form, sound, smell, taste, touch, and wrong perceptions. The sutra talks about the twelve dangers of the great ocean; these are the afflictions that arise as a result of the contact between the six internal and the six external aspects of the senses.

The mind of living beings is afflicted by the intrusion of wrong perceptions that come into it as rivers enter the great ocean. It is like a hungry person who never feels satisfied however much he eats. There is not a single phenomenon, even the subtlest, that is not accepted by the mind. Psychological phenomena enter, leave, and return to the mind as swiftly as a flash of lightning and without interruption.

We cannot see the mind because it has no visible image; we cannot hear the mind because it has no sound. If we go back in time to find it, we do not come across it, because it has no starting point. If we go in pursuit of it, we do not see it, because it does not have a conclusion. This mind is very deep and wonderful. It does not have the smallest mark that could make it visible. Even Brahma, Indra, and the holy ones cannot see clearly the transformation that gives rise to the appearance of the seeds that lie hidden in it, much less ordinary mortals. That is the reason why the mind is called an aggregate. It is like someone who is sowing seeds in the dark. He lifts up a handful of seeds and hundreds of thousands are sown. The person standing alongside him cannot see these seeds being planted, and the sower himself does not know the number of seeds he is planting. When one handful of seeds has been scattered, ten thousand plants could grow up. Similarly, in the time it takes to snap your fingers, nine hundred and sixty recollections can take place in the mind. During one day and one night, thirteen hundred thousand recollections can take place in consciousness and we are not aware of them, just as the person who is planting seeds in the dark. That is why we have to practice attentiveness, binding our mind to our breathing and counting our breaths from one to ten. If the practitioner while counting from one to ten does not forget the count, his mind has begun to have concentration. A small concentration can last for three days and a great concentration for seven days. During this time not a single dispersed thought breaks into the mind of the practitioner. The practitioner sits as still as a corpse. This is called the first meditative concentration.

Meditative concentration is elimination — that is, elimination of the mind that has thirteen hundred thousand unwholesome thoughts, in order to realize eight practices: counting, concentrating, changing, remembering, holding, following, touching, and eliminating. In general these eight practices can be divided into two parts. Following the breathing enables us to concentrate the mind. If we want to follow our breathing easily, we can practice counting our breaths. When the impurities have been destroyed, the mind gradually becomes clear. This is called the second meditative concentration. When you stop counting and place your attention at the end of your nostrils, that is called stopping. If you are successful, then all the impurities of the Three Poisons, the Four Leaks, the Five Hindrances, and the Six Dark Paths are destroyed. At that point the mind is clear and bright, brighter than precious jewels or the light of the moon.

The attention of the mind to sensual desire and the impurities of the mind, which are like mud sticking to a clear mirror, are all wiped clean. Now this mirror is placed on the earth and turned up toward the heavens, and there is no world that it does not reflect. The earth and the sky are endlessly wide but one mirror can embrace them all. Our mind is covered with different kinds of impurities, just as a mirror might be covered by mud. If we are able to meet an enlightened teacher and wipe our mind clean so there is no more mud or dust sticking to it, then it will reflect everything. There will not be the slightest, subtlest thing that does not appear clearly in the mirror. When the impurities are no longer there, the light appears. It is something that happens quite naturally. On the other hand, if afflictions overwhelm the mind and disperse it, then among our ten thousand different thoughts we will not be able to recognize even one. We are like someone sitting in a busy marketplace listening to a hubbub of noise, with many sounds of everyone talking at once. If later we go somewhere else and sit quietly, trying to remember what we have heard, we will not remember a single word.

The reason why our mind is agitated and dispersed is that the unwholesome obstructions have not yet been removed. If we are able to find an undisturbed place to practice, so that our mind can settle down and our thoughts will not be carried away by wrong desires, then we will be able to hear clearly ten thousand words, and we will not lose a single one of them. We can do this because our mind is calm and our thought clear. To practice the silencing of thought and the stopping of the mind by concentrating on the place where the air enters the nostrils is called the third meditative concentration. When we return to ourselves to meditate on our own body from the head down to the feet, we observe all the impurities in our body. We are able to see clearly every pore of our skin and the liquid that exudes from these pores. As a result of this we are able to meditate on the heavens, earth, people, and phenomena. We can meditate on the prosperity and decline of these phenomena, and we will see how phenomena are not permanent but also are not annihilated. At that point our faith in the Three Jewels becomes very solid. Now all darkness and obscurity becomes clarity. That is the fourth meditative concentration.

Making our mind one-pointed, we return to right mindfulness, and all hindrances are destroyed. That is called returning. When ignorance, attachment, and other impurities have been completely pacified, then the mind has no more wrong perceptions. That is called purification. The practitioner has realized the method of mindful breathing when she sees her mind light up with clarity. The practitioner uses this clarity to look deeply. There is no part of the mind that is so dark that it cannot be lit up. Such a practitioner is able to see what has happened for numberless lifetimes before and can also see all the worlds in the present moment, with their people and other phenomena. She can see the Buddhas giving teachings and their disciples learning and practicing. She can observe any world and hear any sound. She has achieved great freedom and is no longer bound by the ideas of permanence and annihilation. She is able to see the immeasurably great, like Mt. Sumeru, contained in the infinitely small, like a pore of the skin. She can master the earth and the heavens and is in control of her own life span. Her spiritual strength is now powerful and courageous. She can defeat an army of the gods and move the three chiliocosms. She can displace ten thousand lands. She can enter the world that cannot be measured or conceived. Her energy is such that Brahma cannot measure it. The spiritual qualities of that person become inestimable, because she has been able to put into practice the Six Paramitas.

Before the Buddha taught this sutra, the worlds of gods and men shook and changed color. For the whole of three days the Buddha dwelt in the mindfulness of breathing, and no one approached him. After that the Buddha gave rise to two bodies: one was the retribution body and the other the transformation body, which is used to explain the true meaning. All the Noble Ones and the Great Beings of the six pairs and the twelve categories agreed to practice these teachings of the Buddha.

There is a bodhisattva who goes by the name An Qing, whose title is Shi Gao. He was once heir to the throne of Parthia. After he abdicated in favor of his uncle, he came to this country. He traveled to many places and finally he came to the capital. He has studied widely, and his knowledge is great. He has gone deeply into every field of learning. His knowledge of the seven schools of thought of our own time is very rich. He has a firm grasp of the art of geomancy, he knows the auspicious marks, he can predict calamities like earthquakes, and he knows the medicinal arts, such as pulse reading. He understands the songs of many species of birds and the calls of the wild animals, and in his heart he includes the great expanse of *yin* and *yang*. Seeing people living blind in the darkness, he felt great compassion. He wanted to develop the range of what they could see and what they could hear, in order to help them see and hear more clearly. It is for them that he has explained the path of the Six Paramitas and has translated and brought to light this *Anapananusmriti Sutra*. Everyone who learns from him can eliminate the pollution of ignorance and can come to live in the light of clarity and purity.

I, Tang Hôi, had hardly reached the age when I could carry wood, when my mother and father passed away. My three ordination teachers, one after the other, also passed away. Whenever I looked up at the clouds in the sky, I could not help but feel deep emotion, and from sadness and love I shed tears. Fortunately, thanks to the merit I still had from former lives, I met three kind friends: Han Lin from Nam Duong, Pi Ye from Ying Chuan, and Chen Hui from Hui Qi. All three of them have a very firm faith. Their aspiration to virtuous conduct is lofty and deep. All three of them are energetic in serving the Dharma, which they do without growing tired. From the time I had the opportunity to be on intimate terms and to discuss the Dharma with them, I realized that our way of working together and our way of thinking is in perfect harmony, and there is no conflict between us. The layman Chen Hui did the work of writing the commentary, and I just gave some assistance by polishing the text, adding a little here and taking away a little there. Obviously I did not take the liberty to introduce into the text things that Master Shi Gao had not taught. However, whatever I say cannot match the meaning of the Buddha. Therefore, I respectfully ask all of you virtuous ones who have clear sight to help me. If you see any place that is incorrect or anything missing, please complete and correct it, so that together we may make clearer the beautiful meaning of the Buddha's teachings.

6 The Practice of Mindful Breathing

IN THE PREFACE to the *Anapananusmriti Sutra,*
Tang Hôi states:

> Meditative concentration is elimination — that is, elimination
> of the mind that has thirteen hundred thousand unwholesome
> thoughts, in order to realize eight practices: counting, concen-
> trating, changing, remembering, holding, following, touching,
> and eliminating.

As an equivalent to the eight practices listed above — counting,
concentrating, changing, remembering, holding, following, touching,
and eliminating — there are the Six Wonderful Dharma Doors created
by the ancestral teachers of the Meditation school. They include:
counting the breath, following the breath, stopping, looking deeply,
returning, and purifying.[1]

The method of counting the breath is used when our minds are
very distracted. We breathe in and we count one, we breathe out and
we count one. We breathe in and we count two, we breathe out and we
count two. We continue counting like this until we reach ten, then we
either go back to one or we count backwards from ten down to one.

---

1 The Six Wonderful Dharma Doors and the eight practices mentioned here are not
found in the original version of the *Anapananusmriti Sutra,* either in the Southern transmission nor the Northern transmission. Southern transmission refers to the Pali Canon.
In this case, the Buddha's teachings went south from the Ganges to Sri Lanka. Northern
transmission refers to the Chinese Canon. In this case, the Buddha's teachings went north
to Kashmir and thence to China.

If we can count from one to ten and back down to one again and our mind does not get distracted, we already have meditative concentration.

When we can count our breath and not lose track of the count, then the second method—following the breath—can be practiced. When we follow the breath, we know exactly at which point our in-breath has arrived and our out-breath has left. We have not mistaken the in-breath for the out-breath, and we have not mistaken the out-breath for the in-breath. Breathing in, we are aware of the in-breath for the entire in-breath. Breathing out, we are aware of the out-breath for the entire out-breath. This is called "following the breath." It is a wonderful practice. In Plum Village we follow the breath as we walk, and sometimes we count the number of steps we make with each in-breath and out-breath.

The text continues:

> Following the breathing enables us to concentrate the mind. If we want to follow our breathing easily, we can practice counting our breaths. When the impurities have been destroyed, the mind gradually becomes clear. This is called the second meditative concentration. When you stop counting and place your attention at the end of your nostrils, that is called stopping. If you are successful, then all the impurities of the Three Poisons, the Four Leaks, the Five Hindrances, and the Six Dark Paths are destroyed.

The Three Poisons referred to are craving, hatred, and ignorance. The Six Dark Paths are unwholesome mental formations of selfishness, harming, anger, hypocrisy, flattery, and arrogance.

The Four Leaks (ashrava) are like streams of water that pull us along with them. The presence of the Four Leaks means that our actions or experiences do not have the nature of true insight and liberation— the possibility still exists of our falling down or turning back, or that the fruits of our actions will create more seeds of delusion in our consciousness. There is still something dripping out, like water from a cracked earthenware jar. The first leak is desire, and refers to the cling-ing and impulsive nature of desire. The second is the attachment to being. The third is wrong views. The fourth is ignorance, which means a lack of clear understanding regarding the true nature of things.

Attachment to being comes about because people have a concept of nonbeing. There are many people who are afraid of nonbeing and for that reason they do their best to grasp hold of being. If we believe that before we were born we did not exist, and that when we die we will become nonexistent again, the fear of nonbeing is very real. If we continue to grasp hold of being, at the time of our death we will fear that from being a "self," a "me," there will be nothing.

Buddhism teaches us that reality is neither "being" nor "nonbeing." We cannot say that before we were born we did not exist; nor can we say that the time of our birth was the beginning of our existence. Therefore when we die, we will not go back to a state of nonexis-tence. Sufficient conditions come together to make it possible for us to manifest. When these conditions are no longer sufficient, we cease to manifest. If we can see that—if our insight goes beyond being and nonbeing—then we will be at peace at the moment of our death.

Wrong views are our wrong perceptions. Our perceptions of birth and death, being and nonbeing, permanence and annihilation, com-ing and going are wrong perceptions. Ignorance is the absence of clarity and awakened understanding. These are the Four Leaks that sweep us along with them, causing us to fear, doubt, and suffer.

When we know how to look deeply we can be released from the Three Poisons, the Four Leaks, the Five Hindrances, and the Six Dark Paths.

THE SIXTEEN BREATHINGS

In the essay "The Way of Realizing Meditation," Tang Hôi teaches a version of the sixteen breathings that is a little different from the sixteen breathings found in the *Anapanasati Sutta* in the Pali Canon and the *Anapananusmriti Sutra* in the Chinese Canon. His version, found below, is almost identical to the Sixteen Breathings in the commentary to the *Greater Anapananusmriti Sutra*[2]:

> The bodhisattva knows how to practice the sixteen methods of mindful breathing in order to make her mind one-pointed and to realize meditative concentration. What are these sixteen methods?
>
> 1. Breathing in and out a long breath, she knows she is breathing in and out a long breath.
>
> 2. Breathing in and out a short breath, she knows she is breathing in and out a short breath.
>
> 3. Breathing in and out and being aware of the body, she knows she is aware of the body.
>
> 4. Breathing in and out and calming the body, she knows she is calming the body.
>
> 5. Breathing in and out in with a pleasant feeling, she knows she has a pleasant feeling.
>
> 6. Breathing in and out with an unpleasant feeling, she knows she has an unpleasant feeling.
>
> 7. Breathing in and out and calming the feeling, she knows she is calming the feeling.
>
> 8. Breathing in and out and not calming the feeling, she knows she is not calming the feeling.
>
> 9. Breathing in and out and feeling happy, she knows she is happy.

2 One version of the *Anapananusmriti Sutra* was translated by An Shi Gao from Sanskrit into Chinese, but that version is no longer extant. All that is left from that version is the commentary which can be found in the Chinese Canon under the title of the *Greater Anapananusmriti Sutra*.

10. Breathing in and out and not feeling happy, she knows she is not happy.

11. Breathing in and out, she sees that all things are impermanent.

12. Breathing in and out, she sees that nothing can be grasped hold of.

13. Breathing in and out, she sees that there is no attachment in her mind.

14. Breathing in and out, she knows she is giving up her perceptions.

15. Breathing in and out, she knows she is giving up her idea of body and life span.

16. Breathing in and out, she knows she has not yet given up her idea of body and life span.

It isn't clear from which of the eighteen Buddhist schools[3] in India this version of the *Anapananusmriti Sutra* comes. This version is basically the same as the one in the Pali Canon and in the *Samyukta Agama* of the Chinese Canon, but there are differences. We can experiment in our sitting meditation with the different versions in order to discover the best way to practice. In the version of the Pali Canon the first and second breathing exercises are as follows:

Breathing in and out a long breath, she knows she is breathing in and out a long breath.
Breathing in and out a short breath, she knows she is breathing in and out a short breath.

---

3 One hundred and forty years after the passing away of the Buddha, Buddhist practitioners were divided into eighteen different schools. Each school had its own canon. However, the only canons that are anywhere near complete are those of the Tamrasatiya school (in Pali) and the Sarvastivada school (translated from Sanskrit into Chinese).

This progression is not natural. Usually at the beginning of a session of sitting meditation our breathing is short and gradually becomes longer rather than the other way around.

In the Chinese version of the *Anapananusmriti Sutra (Samyukta Agama),* the first and second breathing exercises are as follows:

> *Breathing in, he knows he is breathing in. Breathing out, he knows he is breathing out.*
> *Breathing in a long or a short breath, he knows whether it is long or short. Breathing out a long or a short breath, he knows whether it is long or short.*

Here we see that the first two breathing exercises in the Pali version become the second breathing exercise in the version in the *Samyukta Agama.* I have put together three sutras in the *Samyukta Agama* (803, 810, 815) and translated them under the heading of the *Anapananusmriti Sutra.*[4] These three sutras from the Chinese Canon contain all the teachings that are found in the *Anapanasati Sutta* in the Pali Canon with some additional details. These sutras can be very helpful for our practice. In Plum Village we have devised simplified versions of the breathing exercises that have become almost classic, and have benefited many people in their practice. In the book *The Blooming of a Lotus,*[5] several exercises have been developed based on the exercises in the *Anapananusmriti Sutras.* If you wish to develop your studies of the *Anapananusmriti Sutras,* the exercises in *The Blooming of a Lotus* will be helpful to you.

4 See Thich Nhat Hanh, *Breathe! You Are Alive: Sutra on the Full Awareness of Breathing.*
5 See Thich Nhat Hanh, *Blooming of a Lotus: Guided Meditation Exercises for Healing and Transformation* (Boston, MA: Beacon Press, 1993).

7 Elements of Late Buddhist Psychology and the Avatamsaka School in Tang Hôi's Writings

TANG HÔI TAUGHT that the wholesome elements that result from meditative concentration can burn up, destroy, and eliminate the impurities in the mind. When these impurities have been destroyed, our minds become clear naturally, and we are able to see things that we had not seen before. These new insights do not come from outside of us. Our mind is like a mirror that is covered with dust. When it is wiped clean the mirror reflects naturally. This teaching can be found in the *Anguttara Nikaya,*[1] where we find sutras that teach that the essence of our mind is clear. For example, the Buddha says: "O *bhikkhus*, the mind is clear in its essence, but the alien dust of the afflictions makes it clouded. Therefore, when we are able to destroy this alien dust of affliction, the clear aspect of our mind manifests."

In the Preface to the *Anapananusmriti Sutra* we read:

> If you are successful, then all the impurities of the Three Poisons, the Four Leaks, the Five Hindrances, and the Six Dark Paths are destroyed. At that point the mind is clear and bright, brighter than precious jewels or the light of the moon.
>
> The attention of the mind to sensual desire and the impurities of the mind, which are like mud sticking to a clear mirror, are all wiped clean. Now this mirror is placed on the earth and turned up toward the heavens, and there is no world that it does not reflect. The earth and the sky are endlessly wide but

---

1 This is a section of the Buddhist Canon in the Pali language.

one mirror can embrace them all. Our mind is covered with the different kinds of impurities, just as a mirror might be covered by mud. If we are able to meet an enlightened teacher and wipe clean our mind so there is no more mud or dust sticking to it, then it will reflect everything. There will not be the slightest, subtlest thing that does not appear clearly in the mirror. When the impurities are no longer there, the light appears.

The Vijñanavada school of Buddhist psychology had not yet been founded when Tang Hôi wrote the Preface to the *Anapananusmriti Sutra*, although some of the Mahayana sutras had already appeared. For example, we know for certain that Tang Hôi had read the *Prajñaparamita Sutras,* because he himself translated the *Prajñaparamita in Eight Thousand Lines*. He had also read the *Lotus Sutra*. He could also have read the early sutras of the *Avatamsaka* collection, for example the *Dasabhumika (The Ten Bhumis).*[2] It is clear from the Preface to the *Anapananusmriti Sutra* that Tang Hôi knew about the teaching of the multiple layers of causes that was to be explained later in the *Avatamsaka Sutra*.

In the time of Tang Hôi, *The Lion's Roar of Queen Srimala,* the *Mahaparinirvana Sutra,* and the *Lankavatara Sutra* had not yet appeared. We know that the significant works of the Vijñanavada school, like the *Vijñaptimatrata Verses* of Vasubandhu and the *Mahayana-samgrahashastra* of Asanga, Vasubandhu's elder brother, did not yet exist because these two masters lived in the fifth century. Therefore it is very surprising to see the principles of the Vijñanavada school already being expressed in the teachings of Tang Hôi at the beginning of the third century.

The excerpt above refers to the Great Mirror Wisdom, the wisdom that arises when the *alaya* consciousness[3] is transformed and cleaned of the affliction of ignorance. When the afflictions have been

2 The *bhumis* are levels of realization in the practice. The ten levels of practice of a bodhisattva is the subject of the *Dasabhumika Sutra*.
3 Also known as the store consciousness or the eighth consciousness in Buddhist

removed, burned up, and transformed, the alaya consciousness (or store consciousness) becomes a great, wide mirror that is able to reflect the ten directions. If read from a historical point of view, we see that Tang Hôi was in the vanguard of the Vijñanavada school. Although he did not use terminology like "alaya consciousness" or "Great Mirror Wisdom," he is clearly talking about them. When we hear Tang Hôi say, "The earth and the sky are endlessly wide but one mirror can embrace them all," we feel that we are reading the *Avatamsaka Sutra*. This is the teaching of the *Avatamsaka Sutra*—the one containing the all, the one penetrating the all, and the one reflecting the all. Tang Hôi says that we are able to see all the Buddha realms in the ten directions when the mind is purified.

Here Tang Hôi discusses the fourth meditative concentration and the practice of looking deeply:

On the other hand, if afflictions overwhelm the mind and disperse it, then among our ten thousand different thoughts we will not be able to recognize even one. We are like someone sitting in a busy marketplace listening to a hubbub of noise, with many sounds of everyone talking at once. If later we go somewhere else and sit quietly, trying to remember what we have heard, we will not remember a single word.

The reason why our mind is agitated and dispersed is that the unwholesome obstructions have not yet been removed. If we are able to find an undisturbed place to practice, so that our mind can settle down and our thoughts will not be carried away by wrong desires, then we will be able to hear clearly ten thousand words, and we will not lose a single one of them. We can do this because our mind is calm and our thought clear.

psychology, it is the part of consciousness of which we usually have very little awareness. It is where everything is stored in the form of "seeds." These seeds manifest as mental formations and objects of mind when the causes and conditions are sufficient.

The following excerpt gives a feeling of the *Avatamsaka Sutra*. Looking deeply into one pore of the skin of the body, we are able to see all the Dharma realms.

> To practice the silencing of thought and the stopping of the mind by concentrating on the place where the air enters the nostrils is called the third meditative concentration. When we return to ourselves to meditate on our own body from the head down to the feet, we observe all the impurities in our body. We are able to see clearly every pore of our skin and the liquid that exudes from these pores. As a result of this we are able to meditate on the heavens, earth, people, and phenomena. We can meditate on the prosperity and decline of these phenomena, and we will see how phenomena are not permanent but also are not annihilated.

"Not permanent and not annihilated" means the same as "nonbeing and not-nonbeing." If we were to study the *Anapananusmriti Sutra* just from the point of view of the Theravada, we would not be able to see the things that Tang Hôi sees. Tang Hôi learned from the Mahayana tradition and used the *Anapananusmriti Sutra* in the way of a Mahayana bodhisattva—by looking into one pore of the skin and seeing the heavens, the earth, people, things, and the prosperity and the decline of all these phenomena. Looking deeply like this we see that things do not have the nature of being or nonbeing, of arriving or departing, of one or many. Whereas before we were practicing calming and stopping, here we are practicing looking deeply.

> Making our mind one-pointed, we return to right mindfulness, and all hindrances are destroyed. That is called returning. When ignorance, attachment, and other impurities have been completely pacified, then the mind has no more wrong perceptions. That is called purification. The practitioner has realized the method of mindful breathing when she sees her mind

light up with clarity. The practitioner uses this clarity to look deeply. There is no part of the mind that is so dark that it cannot be lit up. Such a practitioner is able to see what has happened for numberless lifetimes before and can also see all the worlds in the present moment, with their people and other phenomena. She can see the Buddhas giving teachings and their disciples learning and practicing.

This is clearly a principle of the *Avatamsaka Sutra.*

She can observe any world and hear any sound. She has achieved great freedom and is no longer bound by the ideas of permanence and annihilation. She is able to see the immeasurably great, like Mt. Sumeru, contained in the infinitely small, like a pore of the skin.

The more we read, the more clearly we see the principles of the *Avatamsaka Sutra:*

She can master the earth and the heavens and is in control of her own life span.

We no longer have the feeling that we are a cork bobbing up and down on the surface of the ocean. Before we were the victims of our life span, now we are masters of the heavens and earth and our life span. We have arrived at what is called "freedom from life span"—we have gone beyond the idea of thinking that we were born at a set time and we will die at a set time. We are born in freedom and we die in freedom, and birth and death are no longer able to touch us—we are the masters of our life span. Eminent Master Tue Trung[4] writes in his "Song of Freedom":"Why should birth and death put pressure on us? They are not able to touch me."

4 A Vietnamese meditation master who died in 1291.

8 The Psychological Basis
of Tang Hôi's Teachings

I N THE VERY FIRST SENTENCE of the Preface to the *Anapananusmriti Sutra*,[1] Tang Hôi says:

> Mindfulness of breathing is the great vehicle used by the Buddhas to save beings who are tossing up and down and drowning in the ocean of great suffering.

He is saying here that the practice of mindful breathing is a Mahayana method because "Mahayana" means "great vehicle," and is thereby giving the *Anapananusmriti Sutra,* which is a basic meditation sutra of the Theravada school, a Mahayana flavor.

The next sentence reads: "There are six kinds of mindfulness of breathing aimed at treating the six senses." As we have seen, the six methods referred to are: counting the breath, following the breath, stopping, looking deeply, returning, and purifying. In Sanskrit the six senses are called the six *ayatanas.* They are made up of the six sense organs: eyes, ears, nose, tongue, body, and mind; and the six objects of sense: form, sound, smell, taste, touch, and objects of mind. The six sense organs are sometimes called the "six internal senses" or "internal fields." The six sense objects are sometimes called "the six external senses" or the "six external fields." When the six internal fields are in contact with the six external fields, an additional six fields are pro-

---

1 *Anapana* means "breathing in and breathing out." *Anusmriti* means "mindfulness." "Anapananusmriti" is therefore translated as "mindfulness of breathing."

duced called the six consciousnesses: eye consciousness, ear con-
sciousness, nose consciousness, tongue consciousness, body con-
sciousness, and mind consciousness. Together they are called the
Eighteen Dhatus or the eighteen fields.[2]

The last of the external fields is objects of mind. Tang Hôi regards
objects of mind as wrong mindfulness because when we perceive an
object of mind, our perception is nearly always wrong perception.

The sutra talks about the twelve dangers of the great ocean;
these are the afflictions that arise as a result of the contact
between the six internal and the six external aspects of the
senses.

When the six internal aspects of the senses are in touch with the
six external aspects, we can become attached to images, sounds, scents,
tastes, touch, and objects of mind, and the attachment becomes an
internal formation. Therefore, the Buddha teaches us to guard our
senses. Our six senses are like six doors, and right mindfulness is like
the sentinel who stands guard at the door. Each of the six senses needs
its own sentinel so that the invaders do not slip in unnoticed and take
over the city. If we live without practicing mindfulness, internal formations will be created and they will enter into the depths of our
consciousness.

The mind of living beings is afflicted by the intrusion of wrong
perceptions that come into it as rivers enter the great ocean. It
is like a hungry person who never feels satisfied however much
he eats.

Tang Hôi bases his meditation teachings on an understanding of
psychology. In the passage above he compares the mind to the ocean

2 The eighteen fields contain the whole of existence. Nothing in the universe can escape
these eighteen fields. In fact, the universe is the eighteen fields.

that receives water from all the rivers that flow into it. This means that when there is contact between the six sense organs and the six sense objects, then images, sounds, and other sense perceptions enter our consciousness like the water from a river entering the sea. When practicing meditation, it is essential to understand our mind—to learn about how our mind is perfumed by habit energy, and how the seeds are maintained in the store consciousness.

Meditation Master Thuong Chieu of twelfth-century Vietnam said: "If the practitioner understands clearly her own mind, then with little effort she will be successful in the practice. If the practitioner knows nothing about her mind, then she will make a great deal of effort to no avail." In Plum Village we base our practice on our observation of the store consciousness and the seeds in store consciousness.[3]

Another analogy Tang Hôi uses to describe the mind is that of a hungry person who never feels satisfied. Imagine a child in New York or Paris who turns on the television whenever she feels like it. Sometimes she watches three or four hours of television a day. While watching the television, she is invaded by countless sounds, images, and emotions, and she feels that she cannot live without television. Many children come to Plum Village and ask: "Is there a television here?" On hearing the answer "no" they are extremely disappointed, "like a hungry person who never feels satisfied." We are always filling our consciousness with sounds, images, and emotions.

Tang Hôi says that the mind is filled with every kind of phenomenon. "There is not a single phenomenon, even the subtlest, that is not accepted by the mind." This is clearly a description of the store consciousness. It is usually assumed that the concept of the store consciousness was first developed in the fifth century by the Vijñanavada school, but here we see that as early as the second century, even before the *Lankavatara Sutra*,[4] Tang Hôi had already developed this concept. The Mahayana sutras that were available to Tang Hôi were the *Greater*

3 For the fundamentals of Buddhist psychology, see Thich Nhat Hanh, *Transformation at the Base: Fifty Verses on the Nature of Consciousness* (Berkeley, CA: Parallax Press, 2001).
4 A late Mahayana sutra which includes many teachings on Buddhist psychology.

and the *Lesser Prajñaparamita Sutras,* the *Lotus Sutra,* the early parts of
the *Avatamsaka* collection called the *Dasabhumika* and *Entering the
Dharma Realms,* the *Vimalakirti-nirdesa,* and the *Surangama-samadhi
Sutra.* Sutras such as *The Lion's Roar of Queen Srimala,* the *Mahaparinirvana* (Mahayana version), the *Lankavatara,* and the *No-Increase
No-Decrease Sutras* had not yet appeared. Although Tang Hôi does
not use the same terminology that the later Buddhist psychologists
used from the fifth century onwards, it is clear that his teachings on
meditation are based on psychology.

> There is not a single phenomenon, even the subtlest, that is
> not accepted by the mind. Psychological phenomena enter,
> leave, and return to the mind as swiftly as a flash of lightning
> and without interruption.
>
> We cannot see the mind because it has no visible image; we
> cannot hear the mind because it has no sound. If we go back
> in time to find it, we do not come across it, because it has no
> starting point. If we go in pursuit of it, we do not see it, because
> it does not have a conclusion.

The function of store consciousness, as described above, is to
receive and hold. The nature of mind is such that we are not able to
see it or hear it. The mind is without image or sound, without beginning and without end. There is a famous gatha in the *Mahayana-samgraha-shastra* of Asanga[5] describing the store consciousness:

> *There is a realm which comes from beginningless time,*
> *It is the refuge place equally for all phenomena.*
> *Because of it all destinies are available.*
> *Nirvana too can be witnessed there.*

5 A master of Buddhist psychology who lived in India at the end of the fifth century C.E.

"Realm" here means the "field" or the "land." "All destinies" refers to the "destinations": god, *ashura,*[6] human, animal, hungry ghost, and hell realms. In the *Mahayana-samgraha-shastra* and in a number of sutras that appeared later, such as the *Lankavatara Sutra,* we find the principle of a consciousness that is without beginning or end and where everything can be found. In the teachings of Tang Hôi this concept of consciousness already exists.

The notion of a store consciousness can already be found in the teachings of the early schools, including the Theravada. During Tang Hôi's time, the term *bhavanga* (literally, "limb of being"), which was used by the Tamrasatiya[7] school, came very close to the concept of store consciousness. Also, the term *mulavijñana,* meaning "root consciousness," was used by the Mahasanghika[8] school. The statement of Tang Hôi that "This mind is very deep and wonderful" refers to what several hundred years later would be called the store consciousness.

These words remind us of the words of Xuanzang who was a Chinese master of Buddhist psychology in the seventh century: *"The three functions of the store are vast. They can never be completely understood."* The three functions of the store are: the subject which stores, the object which is stored, and the attachment to self. "The subject which stores" also means "the capacity to store." The object is the content of the store. The attachment to self refers to the seventh consciousness, the part of consciousness that is responsible for the idea of me and mine, which grasps hold of the contents of store consciousness and holds onto them as the self. In order to maintain the idea of me and mine it gives rise to constant thinking.[9]

Tang Hôi puts it this way:

6 The ashuras are beings who live in conditions of great material wealth, but who are given to great anger. They are sometimes known as the warrior gods.

7 This is a Theravadin school that went to Sri Lanka. The canon of this school is largely extant and forms what is now known as the Pali Canon.

8 This school, called the Majority school, was formed as a reaction to the conservative attitude of the elders. It is usually considered the starting point for the Mahayana.

9 For a complete explanation of store consciousness, see Thich Nhat Hanh, *Transformation at the Base: Fifty Verses on the Nature of Consciousness.*

This mind is very deep and wonderful. It does not have the smallest mark that could make it visible. Even Brahma, Indra, and the holy ones cannot see clearly the transformation that gives rise to the appearance of the seeds that lie hidden in it, much less ordinary mortals. That is the reason why the mind is called an aggregate.[10]

Tang Hôi uses the word "seeds" to denote the object which is stored. Everything that we receive through the gates of the six senses and that enters the consciousness is called a seed.

Tang Hôi describes how seeds enter the mind with an analogy of someone sowing seeds in the dark:

It is like someone who is sowing seeds in the dark. He lifts up a handful of seeds and hundreds of thousands are sown. The person standing alongside him cannot see these seeds being planted, and the sower himself does not know the number of seeds he is planting.

Although it is our own mind and our own sense perceptions that are involved, when seeds enter our mind from the six objects of sense, we are usually not aware of what is happening to us. If we do not practice meditation and guard our six senses, we do not know how many seeds enter our mind or how we are polluting our consciousness with the many images and sounds that come through our six senses every day. Joy, sadness, anger, jealousy, suspicion, and fear manifest and penetrate our consciousness without our knowledge. It is like someone sowing seeds in the dark.

Tang Hôi says:

Similarly, in the time it takes to snap your fingers, nine hundred and sixty recollections can take place in the mind.

10 Aggregate *(skandha)* means a collection of things.

Here the number nine hundred and sixty is not meant to be exact; Tang Hôi is simply expressing the idea that the brain, the emotions, thinking, and perceptions work almost concurrently in order to produce the different states of body and mind.

When Buddhist psychology was systematized in the fifth century, perfuming *(vashana)* and manifestation *(vijñapti)* were described as being inconceivable and imperceptible. Here Tang Hôi is talking about the same thing, although he does not use the terms perfuming and manifestation.

An example of perfuming is when we are learning a new song. The first time we hear the song, the tune enters our consciousness. Then when we begin to sing the song, the notes perfume our consciousness a second time. When we sing it again, the perfuming takes place a third time. When the seeds have been perfumed sufficiently, then we can sing the song on our own without anyone helping us.

This perfuming takes place in an inconceivable way, in an incalculable way. In our daily life our unwholesome and wrong perceptions constantly perfume our consciousness without us knowing anything about it. It is much like placing jasmine flowers in with tea leaves and putting a lid on the container. Three or four days later, the tea will have absorbed the perfume of the jasmine flowers. In the same way, our consciousness also absorbs impressions, and this gives rise to habit energies. This is the perfuming and the manifestation that cannot be conceived. Imagine a child standing on a chair while her mother is dressing her. Suddenly the child says something that amazes her mother. She says: "What an extraordinary child!" The child has heard her mother say this sentence many times and can now repeat it. Like a seed that has been perfumed, the words automatically manifest. This is what is meant by "manifestation that cannot be conceived."

"We cannot see the mind because it has no visible image; we cannot hear the mind because it has no sound." When Tang Hôi says this, we are reminded of the teaching in the *Thirty Vijñaptimatrata Verses: "Inconceivable is the receiving, maintaining, and manifestation of consciousness" (asamviditaka-upadi sthana Vijñaptikan ca tat).* In *Trans-formation at the Base: Fifty Verses on the Nature of Consciousness,* com-posed by Thich Nhat Hanh to make Buddhist psychology readily accessible in the twenty-first century, there is the line: *"The mind is the earth where seeds are sown."* These seeds are maintained in the mind, which is called the store.

Tang Hôi tells us how to protect ourselves:

> During one day and one night, thirteen hundred thousand rec-ollections can take place in consciousness and we are not aware of them, just as the person who is planting seeds in the dark. That is why we have to practice attentiveness, binding our mind to our breathing and counting our breaths from one to ten.

The method that we can use to recognize the seeds that are being sown in our consciousness is to "practice attentiveness, binding our mind to our breathing and counting our breaths from one to ten." If we do not take hold of our breathing and make ourselves present in the moment, then how can we recognize the seeds that are being sown in our consciousness? If we practice mindful breathing as taught in the *Anapananusmriti Sutra,* we can learn to transform what is hap-pening in our minds.

Practicing mindful breathing during sitting and walking medita-tion, and during all our daily activities, is a wonderful way to recog-nize what is happening in the present moment. It is the best way to recognize the seeds that are being sown and watered in our minds. This is called "guarding the six senses by way of mindfulness of breathing."

From this text it is clear that Tang Hôi practiced and taught the basic meditation sutras of the Theravada, such as the *Sutra on the Full Awareness of Breathing,* and that he applied the methods of the Mahayana in his teaching. It is also clear that Buddhism in Jiaozhou in the second and third centuries came from India and that it was Mahayana Buddhism. When Tang Hôi left Jiaozhou and went to teach in Dong Wu, he also taught meditation according to the Mahayana there. Today when we use the meditation sutras of the Theravada and practice them in the light of the Mahayana, we are not doing anything new, we are just following what Tang Hôi did many centuries ago.

APPENDICES

The Preface to the Book
Dispelling Doubts by Mouzi

(From *A History of Vietnamese Buddhism, Vol. 1,*
by Thich Nhat Hanh, published by La Boi, Saigon, 1973)
Translated from Chinese by Thich Nhat Hanh

I, MOUZI, am intrigued by scriptures and their commentaries. There is no book great or small that does not intrigue me. Although I do not like war, I still read books about war strategy. Although I do not believe in the immortal gods, I have read books about them.

After King Han Lingdi passed away, the people rose up in revolt, and only Jiaozhou was peaceful. All those who left the north came to Jiaozhou. The majority of them believed in the worship of the gods, fasting, and the elixir of life. At that time there were many scholars in Jiaozhou. I often took out *The Five Classics* and asked these scholars questions about them. But none of the religious experts and magicians were able to answer these questions to my satisfaction.

My mother and I came to Jiaozhou as refugees, and at age twenty-six I went to Shang Wu to be married. When the governor Shi Xie heard that I had scholarly leanings, he offered me a governmental post. At that time I was still young, and my heart was in studying. I also saw that the times were disturbed, and I had no desire to be a mandarin, so I declined. At that time the local officials in the Han Empire were all suspicious of each other; they were in disharmony and did not communicate well with each other. When the governor saw that I had studied widely and knew many things, he wanted me to go to Jingzhou. I thought that it would be easy enough to decline this honor, but it is difficult to decline an important mission. Therefore, I was prepared to go. The local official, however, who was aware of my scholarly talents, did not find an office for me at that time, and I used my ill-health as an excuse not to go.

The younger brother of the local official, who had been the governor of Yu Zhang, had been murdered by the general responsible for the transportation of rations, whose name was Zha Rong. The local official ordered the military officer Liu Chan to lead an army to Yu Zhang, but he was afraid that the powerful local mandarins would be suspicious of his intentions and block the army.

The local official invited me to come to his residence and said: "My brother was killed by a rebel, and the pain I feel cuts into my flesh and bones and heats my heart and liver. I want to order the military officer Liu to go there, but I am afraid that along the frontier they will be suspicious, and it will not be possible to pass through. You are perfectly equipped from a military and a civil point of view. You have skills in answering questions, so I want you to go to Lingleng and Guiyang and find a way to pass through."

I replied: "For a long time I have eaten your food, and the time of our friendship is long. When it is necessary, the hero should forget his person in order to give his services." I immediately prepared to leave. However, just at that time my mother passed away, and I could not go.

After thinking about the matter properly, I considered that I had been given this mission because of my skills in reasoning. In fact, in times of trouble like these, it is not advisable to show one's face. Then I remembered that Lao Tzu taught that the holy, talented, and wise improve themselves and maintain the true principle. Nothing can sway their deep aspiration. The people cannot disturb their happiness, kings and princes cannot force them to be subjects, the nobility cannot force them to be their companions. That is something very precious. So I sharpened my aspiration to follow the Buddhist path. I also studied Lao Tzu and took the wonderful mystery of life as good wine and *The Five Classics* as my musical instrument. Most people in the world are not aware of this and say that I have betrayed *The Five*

Classics and follow a heretical path. In truth, to open my mouth to argue with them is to go against the path, but if I am silent it looks as if I am powerless. So I took up my pen and ink and composed the sacred and good words that prove and explain the things that I believe. That is what the book *Dispelling Doubts* is about.

APPENDIX TWO

Master Tang Hôi

(Excerpt from *Biographies of High Monks* by Huy Hao)
Translated into Vietnamese by Thich Nhat Hanh

T ANG HÔI'S ANCESTORS on his father's side were Sogdian, but for
many generations his family had lived in India. His father was a
merchant who traveled to Jiaozhou and finally took up residence
there. When he was just ten years old, both his mother and father
passed away. After the obsequies, he became a monk and practiced
very diligently. He was refined, eager to learn, and extremely intelligent. Not only was he knowledgeable in the Buddhist *Tripitaka*,
but he was also widely learned in *The Six Classics*.[1] He studied nearly
all the arts, including astronomy and divination. He firmly grasped
the art of prose writing and studied the art of government, which is
aimed at helping all beings.

At that time, King Sun Quan had taken control of the area called
Jiangzuo. In this area Buddhism was not prohibited. Before that, the
layman Zhi Qian, a native of Indoscythia whose title was Gong Ming
and who also had the name Yue, was making a pilgrimage through
China. Even earlier, in the time of Kings Wandi and Lingdi of the Han
dynasty, someone by the name of Lokaksemo had translated many
sutras. Zhi Liang, with the title Ky Minh, had come to study with Chi
Sam. In time Chi Khien studied with Chi Luong.

Zhi Qian had a very wide knowledge of the sutras. There was no
sutra that he had not studied. He had also studied and practiced nearly

---

1 These are the essential texts of Confucianism. They are usually known as *The Five Classics* because the scripture on music is no longer extant.

all the worldly arts and sciences. He read any book he could get hold of and was fluent in the six languages spoken in China. He was tall, thin, and dark. The whites of his eyes were large, but the pupils were yellow. People of his time often said that, although his eyes are yellow and he is thin, his head is a big sack of knowledge. At the end of the reign of Han Hien Ti, because of the disturbances, Zhi Qian escaped south to the land of Wu. King Sun Quan heard that Qian was talented and learned, so he invited him to the palace. The king was very happy to see him. He conferred on him the duties of doctor, and invited him to teach the prince. Zhi Qian and others, like Wei Yua, did everything they possibly could to support the regime. Because Zhi Qian was a foreigner, the records of Wu do not say anything about him.

Zhi Qian saw that although a large number of sutras were still extant, few had been translated from Sanskrit. Because he was a linguist, he collected many sutras in Sanskrit and translated them into Chinese. From the year 222 C.E. until 252–53 C.E. he translated forty-nine sutras, including the *Vimalakirti,* the *Prajñaparamita in Eight Thousand Lines,* the *Dhammapada,* the *Sutra on the Original Arising of the Auspicious,* etc. He was able to summarize the sacred meaning and express his thoughts in elegant prose. Relying on the theme of the *Amitayus Sutra,* he composed a liturgy of praise called *Verses on the Bodhicitta.* He also wrote a commentary on the sutra *Understanding the Roots of Birth and Death.* All these works are still in circulation.

At this time the land of Wu was beginning to receive the Buddhadharma, but the teachings were hardly complete. Therefore, Tang Hôi decided to develop the Buddhadharma by establishing a native temple in the Jiangzuo area. Carrying a meditation master's cane, he went on foot to Dong Wu. In the year 247 C.E. he arrived in Jianye, built a thatched hut, set up a statue of Buddha, and began to practice there. That was the first time that the people of Wu had seen a monk. Seeing a monk but not knowing what religion he belonged to, they suspected that it was a heresy.

You Bi told the king: "A foreigner has come to our land. He calls himself a monk. His face and his clothes are different from everyone else's. This is something that should be looked into."

King Sun Quan said: "Once King Ming Ti of the Han dynasty had a dream in which he saw a god called by the name of Buddha. That monk could be a practitioner of that religion."

Then the king summoned Tang Hôi and asked: "Does your religion have spiritual power?"

The master replied: "The Tathagata passed away one thousand years ago, but his relics that are left behind have a marvelous and immeasurable power of light. In the past King Ashoka built eighty-four thousand stupas to increase the virtue of the teachings of the Buddha."

King Sun Quan thought this was an excessive boast, and he immediately told Tang Hôi: "If you can get me a relic like that, then I promise that I will build you a stupa where you can worship. But if what you say is false, then the government has laws to deal with you."

Tang Hôi made an agreement to produce a relic in seven days. Speaking to his disciples, he said: "Whether the right Dharma flourishes here or not depends on this. If we put our whole heart and mind into the deep aspiration to be successful now, we will not have cause to regret it in the future."

The master and his disciples organized a retreat where they fasted. They put a bronze vessel on a pedestal, lit incense, and prostrated to invite the relic to come. When seven days had passed and the relic had not appeared, Tang Hôi asked for an extension of seven days.

When after that time still no relic appeared, King Sun Quan said: "This is a real hoax and a slight to the king." Having spoken, he was determined to punish them.

Tang Hôi asked for seven more days, and the king granted them to him. Tang Hôi said to his disciples: "Confucius said, 'The king has died. How can the path not be found within us here?' The miracle should have happened; it is only because we do not have enough faith. If we do not have the deep aspiration to succeed, then we cannot expect the king to support us in any way. It is time for us to vow that if the sacred relic is not realized, we will be ready to die."

When the afternoon of the seventh day of the third week came and still nothing had happened, fear spread amongst the disciples. But at the beginning of the fifth watch, there was a clinking sound in the vase, and Master Tang Hôi himself went to look. He found that a relic had appeared in the vase. The next morning the Master sent someone to present the relic to the king. King Sun Quan summoned the whole court to come and look at it. Everyone there saw a halo of five colors shining in the vase. The king held the vase in his hands and tipped it so that the relic fell onto a bronze tray. In the place where the relic hit the bronze tray, the tray broke.

The king became afraid. He stood up and said: "This is a rare and auspicious event."

Master Tang Hôi came forward and said: "The spiritual power of this relic is not just the light that shines out from it. This relic when set on fire does not burn, and when hit with a diamond pestle does not break."

The king ordered that it be tested. Master Tang Hôi made a deep aspiration: "The Dharma cloud has just spread out across the sky. Ten thousand people are expecting the grace of the Dharma rain. So I ask the relic to manifest its divine nature in order to show its sacred power."

The relic was placed on an iron anvil and a strong man was asked to smash it with a hammer. Both the anvil and the hammer were broken into pieces, but the relic remained intact. King Sun Quan was very impressed, and he decided to have a stupa built where the relic could be revered. Since this was the first time that this land had a Buddhist temple, the place was given the name "First Temple" and the whole complex was called "The Buddha's Center." It was due to this event that from then on the Buddhadharma began to flourish in Jiangzuo.

When King Sun Hao ascended to the throne and held power, his policies were harsh and tyrannical. Not only did he give orders to destroy places of worship where superstition was practiced, but he also destroyed Buddhist temples.

The king would ask: "Where does this temple come from? If I

judge the teachings and practice of the temple to be correct and in agreement with what has been written by the holy ones, then I will allow it to continue its activities. If its teachings and practice do not really have the essence of the Confucian path, then it will have to be burnt and destroyed in the same way as other places that practice superstition."

His mandarins advised him against it, saying: "The power of the Buddha is not the same as the miracles of the deities. It was because Master Tang Hôi performed a miracle in effecting a relic that your father, the king, gave an order to build this temple. If now, out of thoughtless judgment, we destroy the temple, then we fear that in the future we will regret it."

Sun Hao immediately ordered Zhang Yu to go to the temple and question Master Tang Hôi. Zhang Yu was very eloquent, and he questioned Master Tang Hôi about almost everything. The patriarch answered eloquently, appropriately, and directly to the interrogation that lasted from early morning to late at night, and Yu was not able to find any fault with his answers. When Zhang Yu left the temple to go home, Master Tang Hôi went outside to bid farewell to him at the gate. At that time, next door to the temple, there was a place of super-stitious worship.

Zhang Yu asked: "If your teachings and practice are as wonderful as you say they are, why don't these people who reside close by come to be taught by you?"

Master Tang Hôi said: "When there is thunder in the sky, even if it loosens the rocks on the mountain, a deaf person cannot hear it. The reason is not because the sound of thunder is not loud. When the wonderful first principle has been penetrated, then even something that is one thousand miles away is as close as home. If there are obsta-cles in the mind, then although they lie so close to each other, the liver and the spleen seem to be as distant from each other as the land of Zhou[2] is distant from the land of Yue."

2 A part of China.

Zhang Yu went back to the palace and praised Tang Hôi to the king: "I am not able to keep up with Tang Hôi, because he is so talented and intelligent. May your majesty judge the matter for himself and take Tang Hôi by force." The king assembled the court and had a carriage sent to bring Tang Hôi to the palace.

After inviting the patriarch to be seated, the king asked him: "Isn't it true that while Buddhism teaches about retribution of unwholesome and wholesome deeds, Confucianism teaches filial piety and altruism?"

Master Tang Hôi replied: "If the king teaches the people to live according to filial piety and altruistic love, then the red crow will fly in and the five elders will manifest.[3] If you teach the virtue of altruism in order to nourish living beings, then a spring of sweet water will come up from the ground, and the rice crop will multiply. Wholesome things produce omens, and unwholesome things do the same. If you act in an unwholesome way and you hide your deeds, not letting anyone know about them, then the spirits will punish you. If you act in an unwholesome way and let others know about it, then humans will punish you. *The Book of Changes* says: 'The family that stores up wholesome deeds will have much happiness in the future,' and the scripture called *Thi* says: 'To pray for happiness by upright action is to not go astray,' which means the same thing. The ways of Confucianism are like the teachings of Buddhism."

The king said: "If that is so, the teachings of Zhu Gong and Confucius are enough to light the way for the world. We do not need Buddhism as well."

Tang Hôi replied: "The teachings of Confucius and Zhu Gong only present an outline of the truth, while Buddhism takes us into the wonderful and deep nature of the truth. Buddhism teaches that to act unwholesomely results in suffering for a long time in the hell realms, and to act wholesomely will result in long-lasting happiness in paradise. This is taught in order to encourage people in the wholesome

3 The red crow was an auspicious sign which appeared when King Zhou took power. The five elders are an auspicious sign that appeared when King Yao assumed power.

and discourage them from the unwholesome. Is this not an enormous undertaking?" At that point the king could no longer find fault with Tang Hôi. However, although the king had heard the right Dharma, he was not able to change his violent behavior.

One day while the king's soldiers were making a garden behind the palace, they dug up a gold statue of the Buddha that was more than six feet high. When they brought it to show the king, the king ordered that it be placed in the latrine. There he made fun of it with his companions and urinated on it. No sooner had he done this than his whole body, especially the testicles, began to swell, and he cried out until his cries penetrated the heavens.

A mandarin who practiced the art of divination said: "This has happened because you have offended a great spiritual power. If you do not pray and pay respects in all the temples, you will never be cured of your sickness."

A lady-in-waiting who had been practicing Buddhism saw the king's suffering and said to him: "Your majesty, have you been to the Buddhist temple to pray for merit yet?"

The king lifted his head and asked: "Is the spiritual power of the Buddha very great?"

The lady-in-waiting said: "Buddha has the greatest spiritual power of all." The king roused himself and told her everything that had happened. Right away the lady-in-waiting brought the statue of the Buddha from the latrine and placed it in the palace. Using perfumed water, she bathed the statue tens of times, and burned sandalwood in front of it. As she uttered words of repentance, the king hit his head on a cushion to acknowledge his fault. Soon his sickness began to lessen. He immediately ordered a messenger to go to the temple to ask after the well-being of the monks there and to invite Tang Hôi to come and give a Dharma talk.

Tang Hôi returned with the messenger to the palace. The king asked him to talk about the principles of retribution for wrongdoing and goodness. The patriarch proceeded to present the essence of the teachings to the king. The king, who was by nature intelligent, felt very happy when he understood the deep meaning, and asked Tang Hôi to talk about the monastic precepts. Tang Hôi believed that the precepts were something very sacred, and that they should not be expounded on before a worldly person. Therefore, he explained the origin and practice of only 135 of the 250 precepts to the king. These 135 precepts are concerned with fine manners and are practiced daily by monks when walking, standing, lying down, and sitting in daily life, in a way that all their actions are directed to the benefit of living beings. When the king saw the love, compassion, and fine manners that lay behind these precepts, wholesome aspects arose in his own mind, and, with all sincerity, he asked to receive and practice the Five Mindfulness Trainings. Ten days later his sickness disappeared and he was completely healed.

Then the king allowed the buildings of the First Temple, where Tang Hôi lived, to be repaired and made more beautiful. He also commanded everyone in the royal family to follow the Buddhadharma. Tang Hôi frequently came to the palace and taught the right Dharma in the Wu court. However, as the mind and emotions of the king were such that it was difficult for him to penetrate the wonderful deep meaning of the teachings, Tang Hôi only taught about wholesome and unwholesome action to open up the heart and the intellect of the king.

In the First Temple Tang Hôi translated four of the *Jataka Tales,*[4] he also translated the *Prajñaparamita in Eight Thousand Lines, The Collection on the Six Paramitas,* and *The Collection of Examples.* In all these scriptures both the letter and the meaning are exact, and he expresses the spirit of the teachings. He also composed a work on nirvana, which is a chant of praise. The melody and words of this work are both deep and powerful, and it is a model for our age. He also wrote a commentary and the preface to the *Anapananusmriti,* the *Ugradattaparipriccha,* and *The Tree of the Bodhisattva Path.* His prose is elegant and the meaning is deep. These scriptures are extant in our own time. In

4 These are stories concerning former lives of the Buddha told by the Buddha himself. They are included in *The Collection on the Six Paramitas* by Master Tang Hôi.

the fourth month of the year 280 c.e., King Sun Hao abdicated the throne in favor of the Tan dynasty. In the ninth month of that year, Tang Hôi fell ill and passed away.

In the year 326 c.e. in the reign of King Jing Chendi, Su Jun led an uprising and burned down the stupa that Tang Hôi had built. The minister of public works, He Chong, reconstructed the stupa. Zhao Yu, the general of the army, who had never encountered the right Dharma in his life, from time to time expressed scorn for the Three Jewels. When he came to the First Temple he said to the monks there: "For a long time I have heard the rumor that this stupa gives out a light. This seems to me like a lie. It is not something I can believe. If I myself were to see that light, then I wouldn't have any reason to criticize it anymore." As soon as he had finished speaking, a rainbow of five colors shone out from the stupa, lighting up the whole temple. Zhao Yu shook, and the hair stood up on his head. He developed faith and respect and had yet another small stupa built to the east of the temple. All this was because of the spiritual power of the great beings whose teachings had been practiced in the temple and also because of the power of the awakened Master Tang Hôi. People of his time drew portraits and made statues of him that have been handed down to our own time. Sun Chuo wrote a gatha to be placed under one of these portraits. He wrote:

> Noble silence and solitude
> Was his path.
> With the mind of a free person
> And emotions unattached,
> He brought a lamp to shine the way.
> He was able to awaken people.
> Overcoming all obstacles he went far,
> Never caught in worldly things.

There is a note that says it was Sun Hao, not Sun Quan, who ordered that the relic be hit with a hammer. However, we know that when Sun Hao was about to destroy the temple, his advisors reminded him that when his father had the temple built Master Tang Hôi had performed a miracle by producing the relic. This tells us that the relic came into existence during the reign of Sun Quan. Most accounts of this story say that it happened in the time of Sun Hao.

The Beginnings of the Meditation School of Vietnam

(Excerpt from *A History of Vietnamese Buddhism, Vol 1,*
by Thich Nhat Hanh, published by La Boi, Saigon, 1973)
Translated by Sr. Annabel Laity

This book was written by Thich Nhat Hanh when he was teaching at the École des Hautes Études at the Sorbonne in Paris. It is three volumes and spans the time from the first century B.C.E. until 1963.

THE HISTORY OF BUDDHIST MEDITATION in Vietnam begins with Tang Hôi at the beginning of the third century. Master Tang Hôi was a brilliant patriarch of the Vietnamese Buddhist Meditation school and was also the one who brought Buddhist meditation to southern China and developed it there.

His father, a merchant who was Sogdian by birth, came to live in Jiaozhou. Tang Hôi was born in the land of Jiaozhou, and his mother and father died when he was only ten years old. We do not know who was responsible for his upbringing after his parents passed away. But when he was older, he became a monk. He studied and practiced with great diligence *(Biographies of High Monks)* and was proficient in Sanskrit and Chinese. We also do not know who his religious teachers were or whether, among the council of ten who transmitted the full monastic ordination to him, there were any monks from India. Among his works is a collection of poetry on the subject of nirvana, which consists of verses translated from Sanskrit. *The Collection on the Six Paramitas* that he wrote is in a very correct and elegant Chinese prose, and is evidence that his command of Chinese was that of a native of China. Born in Jiaozhou, Tang Hôi more than likely used the language spoken there, which was the precursor of present day Vietnamese.

The book *Biographies of High Monks* says that he came to Nanking, which was then the capital of the kingdom of Wu, in the year 247 C.E. and he died in the year 280. Thus he lived in China for thirty-three years. Many people thought that his writings and translations were done in China, but actually he had already completed an important part of his work in Jiaozhou.

In Tang Hôi's Preface to the *Anapananusmriti Sutra* there is proof that he was writing before the year 229 C.E., which means he was teaching Buddhism in Jiaozhou. The evidence is a detail he wrote about An Shi Gao, the translator of the *Anapananusmriti Sutra:* "There is a bodhisattva who goes by the name An Qing, whose title is Shi Gao. He was once heir to the throne of Parthia. After he abdicated in favor of his uncle, he came to this country. He traveled to many places and finally he came to the capital." The capital referred to here is Luoyang. It was in Luoyang that An Shi Gao translated many sutras in the second half of the second century. If Tang Hôi's preface had been written after 229 C.E., the capital would have been Jianye, not Luoyang, because after Wu Sun Quan proclaimed himself king, Vietnam was a province of Dong Wu (whose capital was Jianye) and not of Bei Wei (whose capital was Luoyang).

This important detail gives us another historical insight. The sutras that An Shi Gao translated in Luoyang were brought to and circulated in Jiaozhou at the time Tang Hôi was teaching and practicing there. These sutras, such as the *Anapananusmriti Sutra,* were brought south by Buddhist followers who came as refugees from Luoyang. Among those Buddhists was the layman Chen Hui, a disciple of An Shi Gao, whom Tang Hôi met and worked with in commenting on the *Anapananusmriti Sutra.* We could say that it was Chen Hui himself who brought this sutra south from Luoyang.

While in Luoyang, An Shi Gao had translated a number of sutras on meditation, like the *Anapananusmriti* and the *Skandha-dhatu-ayatana.*

These sutras belong to the Meditation school but are sometimes regarded as Hinayana. It was Tang Hôi who introduced these sutras in the Mahayana spirit. He compiled *The Collection on the Six Paramitas* and developed dhyana practice in the Mahayana spirit. According to The *Catalogue of Buddhist Books* (730), he also translated the *Ashtasahashrika Prajñaparamita,* the earliest version of the *Prajñaparamita Sutra* to appear. Thus, at the beginning of the third century, Buddhism in Vietnam was Mahayana Buddhism with a mystical and meditational tendency. The fact that Zhi Gang Liang translated the *Saddharmapundarika Samadhi Sutra* in Jiaozhou in the second half of the third century also points to that conclusion.

We do not know all the works that were translated and composed by Tang Hôi. In the index of scriptures made by Dao An, there are a number of translated works listed without the names of the translators. However, in later indexes, these translations are attributed to An Shi Gao. It is possible that a number of them were translated by Tang Hôi. The works that we know were collated or composed by Tang Hôi are as follows:

The *Anapananusmriti Sutra,* translated by An Shi Gao, commentary by Chen Hui and Tang Hôi, preface by Tang Hôi

The *Ugradatta-paripriccha Sutra,* translated by An Yuan, commentary and preface by Tang Hôi

The Tree of the Bodhisattva Path Sutra, translated by Zhi Qian, commentary and preface by Tang Hôi

The Essence of the Six Paramitas, collated by Tang Hôi (no longer extant)

Verses on Nirvana, collated by Tang Hôi (no longer extant)

The *Prajñaparamita in Eight Thousand Lines,* translated by Tang Hôi (no longer extant)

The Collection on the Six Paramitas, collated by Master Tang Hôi

The Collection on the Six Paramitas is a very special work. If we examine the language and the content of the work, it is quite clear that it was not translated from Sanskrit. It was composed and collated by Master Tang Hôi. In it there are extracts from many different sutras, and there are sections, such as the one on meditative concentration, that were wholly composed by Tang Hôi. Altogether there are eight volumes. The first three volumes are devoted to the paramita of giving, and each of the other five volumes is devoted to one of the other five paramitas. In each volume there are many extracts translated from the sutras. For example, in the chapter on the paramita of giving there are extracts from *The King of Benares, The Prince Vishvantara, Sudhana,* and *The Buddha Proclaims the Four Natures.*

Tang Hôi's teachings on meditation had a deep influence on the transmission of the sutras. *Biographies of High Monks* records the story of how An Shi Gao left a small velvet bag with a message in it that read as follows: "The chief of those skilled in the way of practice is the layman Chen Hui; the chief of those skilled in the meditation sutras is the bhikshu Tang Hôi. The meaning transmitted by the layman Chen Hui gives value to my study of the way, whereas the bhikshu Tang Hôi transmits and teaches the meditation sutras." This story gives us an idea of the work of Tang Hôi and Chen Hui in spreading the way of meditation, at first in Jiaozhou and after that in the region of Jiangzuo.

In the Preface to the *Anapananusmriti Sutra* Tang Hôi writes: "The layman Chen Hui did the work of writing the commentary, and I just gave some assistance by polishing the text, adding a little here and taking away a little there." Tang Hôi also says that the corrections he made conformed with the spirit of the way of practice of An Shi Gao, and that he did not take the liberty of adding things that were not in this spirit. But these are only words of self-effacement to show respect for the teacher of his colleague. Tang Hôi had, in truth, infused the meditation study of An Shi Gao with the spirit of Mahayana. Along with Chen Hui, there were two other laymen who may also have been students of An Shi Gao at that time—Han Lin and Pi Ye.

It is notable that all the students of An Shi Gao were laymen, including An Xuan and Yan Fu Tiao. In the Preface to the *Anapananusmriti Sutra,* Tang Hôi calls Chen Hui, Han Lin, and Pi Ye "three kind friends," and in the Preface to the *Ugradatta-paripriccha Sutra,* he calls An Xuan and Yan Fu Tiao "two good men." It is not known whether or not at a later time Yan Fu Tiao took the novice ordination. He did write a book called the *Ten Wisdoms of the Novice in Verse.* It is clear that Chen Hui told Tang Hôi how sutras were translated in Luoyang. Tang Hôi says in the Preface to the *Ugradatta-paripriccha Sutra* that An Xuan translated the text orally, and Yan Fu Tiao, who was a native of China, wrote the translation down. That, at any rate, is the way the *Ugradatta- paripriccha Sutra* was translated.

THE TEACHINGS OF TANG HÔI ON MEDITATION

The term "meditative concentration" (dhyana) is mentioned once in the *Sutra of Forty-Two Chapters.* The translators of this sutra used other words to render the meaning of the four meditative concentrations, like "to practice the path." The sutra mentions "observing the heavens and the earth to remember impermanence." This is a method of meditation called the contemplation on impermanence. In *Dispelling Doubts,* Mouzi does not mention meditative concentration. This book is much more concerned with presenting Buddhism to Taoists and Confucianists, whereas the *Sutra of Forty-Two Chapters* is a pillow book for Buddhist monks. Sutras teaching meditative concentration that were brought from Luoyang at the beginning of the third century and the Mahayana studies of Tang Hôi made Buddhist meditation a living reality in Vietnam and south China in the third century.

For Tang Hôi, meditation was not only knowing the methods of practice but also understanding the mind. In the Preface to the *Anapananusmriti Sutra,* Tang Hôi writes: "Similarly, in the time it takes to snap your fingers, nine hundred and sixty recollections can take place in the mind. During one day and one night, thirteen hundred thousand recollections can take place in consciousness and we are not aware of them, just as the person who is planting seeds in the dark. That is why we have to practice attentiveness, binding our mind to our breathing and counting our breaths from one to ten."

"Anapana" means breath. "Anusmriti" means to give our attention—to "collect the mind" and "concentrate on." So "anapananusmriti" is the method of attentiveness to breathing in order to master the mind. There are six methods called the "Six Wonderful Dharma Doors":

1. Counting the breath: You adjust the posture of the body to make it stable and count the breaths from one to ten. You concentrate the mind on counting to put an end to dispersion and enter meditative concentration.

2. Following the breath: You are aware at every instant of the in-breath and out-breath. You no longer count, you just follow the breath.

3. Stopping: You practice stopping and silencing.

4. Contemplation: Although you have realized concentration, you do not yet have awakened understanding. It is necessary to contemplate the mind, the five skandhas, and wrong perceptions, such as ideas of a self or what belongs to the self, in order to develop awakened understanding.

5. Returning: You return to yourself and observe the body and the mind in order to end the dualism between subject and object and destroy attachment to self.

6. Purification: The nondiscrimination between subject and object is not yet the final breakthrough. The practitioner should not become attached to it. She needs to go beyond this state, so that awakened understanding and true clarity can be wholly revealed.

Master Tang Hôi defines mind as that which has no image, no sound, no before and no after, is profound, wonderful, subtle, and has no trace of a form that can be grasped by the intellect. Brahma, Indra, and the other gods are not able to see it clearly. The seeds of our mind are sometimes dormant and sometimes manifest. In mind, *this* is transformed and becomes *that*. An ordinary person of the world cannot see this transformation process. It is the process that takes place in the store consciousness. Living beings drift and sink, because their minds are pulled along by the six organs and objects of sense and the one million three hundred thousand unwholesome thoughts. The six sense organs are eyes, ears, nose, tongue, body, and mind and are called the inner senses. The six sense objects are form, sound, smell, taste, touch, and object of mind and are called outer senses. The wrong actions coming from our senses are as inexhaustible as the water of ten thousand rivers pouring into the ocean. That is why in dealing with the six sense-fields conscious breathing is necessary to deal with and prevent the arising of unwholesome actions. Tang Hôi continues: "The practitioner has realized the method of mindful breathing when she sees her mind light up with clarity. The practitioner uses this clarity to look deeply. There is no part of the mind that is so dark that it cannot be lit up." (Preface to the *Anapananusmriti Sutra*)

The section that Tang Hôi wrote in *The Collection on the Six Paramitas* concerning dhyana (meditation) is very important. He talks of the four stages of meditation (the four dhyanas) as a way of making our mind upright again.

At the beginning of the Preface to the *Anapananusmriti Sutra* Tang Hôi proclaims: "Mindfulness of breathing is the great vehicle used by the Buddhas to save beings who are tossing up and down and drowning...." This sentence is evidence of the Mahayana tendency in Tang Hôi's meditation practice.

Although Tang Hôi's commentary on the *Anapananusmriti Sutra* is no longer extant, the content of the preface to this sutra and *The Collection on the Six Paramitas* show clearly a Mahayana influence. We do not know with whom Tang Hôi studied meditation in the

Mahayana tradition in Jiaozhou. It was probably not Chen Hui, because Chen Hui, like his master An Shi Gao, followed the Theravada meditation system. We know that Tang Hôi was a translator of the *Astasahashrika Prajñaparamita,* a basic Mahayana sutra, probably the first Mahayana sutra to appear. The *Catalogue of Buddhist Books* mentions this version, although in their prefaces to the *Astasahashrika,* Dao An, Zhi Xun, and Zhi Gang Liang do not mention it. In the second century in Jiaozhou there must have been Indian monks who brought the Mahayana teachings with them, along with the original versions of basic Mahayana sutras such as the *Astasahashrika.* In this sutra the concepts of emptiness and suchness are very carefully explained in full. Thus meditation practice in Vietnam began with the Mahayana meditation teachings, not with the Theravada as in the Luoyang center.

Precisely because he was profoundly influenced by the Mahayana teachings on emptiness and suchness, Master Tang Hôi was able to explain what mind was in the Preface to the *Anapananusmriti Sutra:*

> …[I]t has no visible image; we cannot hear the mind because it has no sound. If we go back in time to find it, we do not come across it, because it has no starting point. If we go in pursuit of it, we do not see it, because it does not have a conclusion. This mind is very deep and wonderful. It does not have the smallest mark that could make it visible. Even Brahma, Indra, and the holy ones cannot see clearly the transformation that gives rise to the appearance of the seeds that lie hidden in it, much less ordinary mortals. That is the reason why the mind is called an aggregate.

According to the author the word "aggregate" is used to translate the Sanskrit "alaya" (store consciousness) and not the Sanskrit word "skandha," because here master Tang Hôi is specifically talking about the mind, and not about the five aggregates that make up the person.

In the Preface to the *Ugradatta-paripriccha Sutra,* Master Tang Hôi speaks of mind as "the source of all objects of mind." This is evidence that Tang Hôi was influenced by the Prajñaparamita school. It looks as if he was also influenced by the Vijñanavada (psychology) school. But at this date there was not yet a true Vijñanavada system of teaching. The *Lankavatara Sutra* that Bodhidharma passed on to Hui Ke at the beginning of the sixth century, which contains psychology teachings, had only appeared in the fourth century. Master Tang Hôi, therefore, seems to have anticipated the later Buddhist psychology teachings. The Mahayana Meditation school differed from the Theravada school in seeing the suchness of the deep and subtle mind as the basis of awakening. Tang Hôi laid the foundations for a Mahayana Meditation school by talking of mind as the source and suchness of all the many objects of mind.

KALASIVI AND MARAJIVAKA

Also in the third century was a monk by the name of Kalasivi (Right Fearlessness), a Scythian who translated the *Saddharma-samadhi Sutra* in Jiaozhou in 255 or 256 C.E. A couple of indices still extant mention another Kalasivi (in which his name is translated as True Joy) as having translated many sutras in Jiaozhou. Paul Pelliot says that the two Kalasivis were one and that the name in Sanskrit should be Kalaruci (in *Toung Pao,* 1923). He cites Phi Truong Phong, extracted from *Lich Dai Tam Bao Ky,* saying that Kalasivi translated the *Twelve Examples Sutra.* The book *Flowers in the Garden of Meditation* gives his name as Chi Cuong Luong (without the last syllable) and, probably due to this, his name was written incorrectly many times afterward either in manuscript or in printed works.

Kalasivi's translation of the *Saddharma-samadhi* was no longer extant after 730. This sutra also belongs to the Mahayana meditation sutras. Samadhi means "meditative concentration." This sutra talks of a concentration called the lotus flower concentration, and in it the concepts of Dharmakaya,[1] magical appearance, and emptiness are examined. A gatha from the sutra reads as follows:

In the Dharmakaya can be found all phenomena.
All are a wonderful magic show of appearance, sometimes drifting,
*   sometimes sinking.*
The afflictions such as attachment, hatred, and ignorance are
*   without form;*
They are like foam appearing on the surface of the water.
We should look at our body and at all phenomena
As dwelling in the place of formless nirvana.
These things come to be because of coming together and falling
*   apart.*
If we can look deeply with our discriminating mind, we shall see
*   clearly the true nature of them all as empty.*

Thus Kalasivi also belonged to the Mahayana Buddhist school and tended toward the meditation teachings.

Apart from Tang Hôi and Kalasivi, in Jiaozhou in the third century there was also Marajivaka, but we have no idea to which school of Buddhism he belonged. *Biographies of High Monks* mentions Marajivaka as someone who was able to perform many miracles, so he may have had a tendency to the Mantrayana or Secret Teachings school. This text records:

Marajivaka was of Indian origin and made pilgrimages to all the civilized and uncivilized countries. He could never settle down in one place. He did things without his disciples and followers knowing in advance. From India he went to Malaysia and then along the sea coast to Jiaozhou and Guang Zhou.

1 The Dharmakaya is the teaching body of the Buddha, which we can see and know even though the historical Buddha is no longer alive. Dharmakaya has come to have the meaning of the wonderful body of reality, available to us when we practice meditation.

Wherever he went he performed miracles, causing the people to admire him greatly. When he came to the Jiang Yang River, the ferrymen saw him in rags and tatters and would not take him across. But when the boat reached the other side he was already standing there. He arrived in Luoyang sometime between 290 and 306, and during the disturbances there he returned to India. The *Phat To Lich Dai Thong Tai* also says that in 294 C.E. a sramana from India came to Luoyang.

DHARMADEVA AND HUE THANG

So far we have not been able to find any documentation concerning Buddhism in Vietnam in the fourth century, and we do not know the details of the meditation practice there in that century. However *The Continuation of Biographies of High Monks* mentions the names of two meditation masters in Jiaozhou in the fifth century, Masters Dharmadeva and Hue Thang. Dharmadeva was from India. He came to Jiaozhou in the middle of the fifth century to teach ways of practicing meditation. Hue Thang was one of his many disciples. *The Continuation of Biographies of High Monks* states:

> Thich Hue Thang was a native of Jiaozhou who resided at the temple on Mount Tien Chau and had visited many mountainous regions. He was of deep understanding, and he read the *Lotus Sutra* continuously throughout the day. He followed the Indian Meditation Master Dharmadeva in order to learn how to practice meditation. Every time he entered meditative concentration he would stay in that concentration for twenty-four hours. When Liuji from Peng Cheng was governor of Nam Hai, he heard about the practice of Hue Thang. When he was about to return to his country, he invited the master to go with him. Hue Thang agreed. When he arrived in Peng Cheng, Hue Thang resided in Youti Temple, where he taught

about the wonderful true nature. He often pretended to be somebody completely stupid, but people who had been with him for a long time respected him greatly. He was admired, especially by students of meditation. In 487 C.E. he moved to Yan Xien which was on Mount Qi Zhong. From when he was young until he was old his mind was pure and upright. He passed away at the age of seventy.

According to *The Continuation of Biographies of High Monks,* we know that Hue Thang specialized in the *Lotus Sutra.* We also know that his meditation teacher, Dharmadeva, who taught him meditation, was a Mahayana meditation master, and therefore Hue Thang's meditation practice must have been from the Mahayana school. From *The Continuation of Biographies of High Monks,* we learn that before Hue Thang went to Yan Xien province in 487 C.E., he had resided at Youti Temple for some time. Therefore he must have been in Dong Wu many years before 487, and Dharmadeva must have gone to Jiaozhou in the middle of the fifth century, before Bodhidharma went to meet King Liang. *Records of the Transmission of the Lamp* by Dao Yuan says that Bodhidharma went to China in 520 and, after his failure with King Liang Wudi, he immediately crossed the river into Bei Wei. However, in the *The Continuation of Biographies of High Monks* Dao Xuan writes: "Bodhidharma in the beginning landed in Nam Viet, a colony of the Song dynasty, and finally crossed the river into Bei Wei." Here Nam Viet may refer to Jiaozhou, which also belonged to the Song dynasty. The Song dynasty (420–447 C.E.) preceded the Qi dynasty (479–501 C.E.).

If in fact Bodhidharma went to Nam Viet at the end of the Song era, it is possible that he went to visit King Liang at the same time as Dharmadeva went to Jiaozhou. Bodhidharma was to become very famous in China, whereas the historical records say virtually nothing about Dharmadeva. There could be two reasons for this. The first is that in the fifteenth century the armies of the Mongols and Ming dynasty from the north burned all the historical records of Vietnam so that not a thing was left. Moreover, the Chinese records of this time say almost nothing about Jiaozhou. The second reason is that meditation practice in the south emphasized the practice and tended to be mystical; only the slightest importance was given to the matter of keeping records about the establishment of different meditation schools.

Tang Hôi came to Jianye in the middle of the third century to teach Buddhist meditation. In the middle of the fourth century in China, Dao An also emphasized meditation and, like Tang Hôi, began to comment on sutras about meditation such as the *Anapananusmriti Sutra* that had been translated by An Shi Gao. Also like Tang Hôi, Dao An studied the *Prajñaparamita Sutras* and was inclined to make meditation a Mahayana practice. Hui Yuan was the successor of Dao An and lived at the end of the fourth century and the beginning of the fifth century. He also emphasized meditation practice and the study of the sutras on meditation. When Hue Thang came from Jiaozhou, there were many Buddhists in Jianye who were attracted to meditation practice. These were the people who were able to see the true value of Hue Thang. In the history of the development of meditation practice in China, there were at least two meditation masters that came from Jiaozhou. They were Tang Hôi and Hue Thang. From the time of Meditation Master Thong Bien of the Ly era until now, there has been the tendency to think that Buddhist meditation practice was brought to Vietnam from China. It was thought that Buddhist meditation practice was introduced into Vietnam at the end of the sixth century by Master Vinitaruci, a disciple of the third patriarch of the Chinese Meditation school. In fact, meditation practice had already begun in Vietnam at the beginning of the third century, and it was Tang Hôi who brought meditation practice to China. Then, in the fifth century, Hue Thang was invited by a district governor to come to China from Jiaozhou and teach meditation practice.

When Vinitaruci went to Vietnam from China, he stayed in Dharma Cloud Temple. This temple was a meditation center before he arrived. In *Flowers in the Garden of Meditation* we learn that Master

Quan Duyen taught meditation practice to many disciples, including Phap Hien, before Master Vinitaruci came. "Master Phap Hien was from Chau Dien. His family name was Do. He was seven feet, three inches tall. In the beginning he studied under the great master Quan Duyen. He received the bhikshu precepts, and every day along with the other disciples of the master he heard teachings on the essential practice of meditation." This points to the fact that meditation practice in Vietnam did not come from China originally. Because neighboring China was a large country with a flourishing culture, the Vietnamese people often felt that anything of value had to come from China. This was especially true during and after the period of colonization. The Vinitaruci, Vo Ngon Thong, and Cao Tang schools all had roots in China. But this does not mean that meditation practice in Vietnam only came from China.

The Importance of Master Tang Hôi in Jianye

Before Master Tang Hôi came to promote the teachings of meditation practice south of the Yangtze, a layman by the name of Zhi Qian had already been there and had translated a number of sutras, such as the *Vimalakirti,* the *Mahaparinirvana,* the *Dhammapada,* the *Verses on the Bodhisattva,* the *Original Arising of the Auspicious,* and *Understanding the Roots of Birth and Death.* In the section of *Biographies of High Monks* that talks about Master Tang Hôi, it is stated that apart from the presence of this layman Buddhism did not have any center in the land of Wu. Zhi Qian was of Scythian origin and was fluent in both Sanskrit and Chinese. He was one of the refugees who fled from the north to Dong Wu. *Biographies of High Monks* also tells us that Master Tang Hôi was the first Buddhist monk to appear in this land, and that the people, especially King Wu Sun Quan, were very suspicious of him. The king put Master Tang Hôi to the test before gaining faith in him, and only then did he bow to receive the Five Mindfulness Trainings. These records also tell us that Master Tang Hôi founded the first Buddhist temple in this land and for that reason the temple was called the First Temple. It says that after Master Tang Hôi arrived the Dharma began to prosper in Jiangnan. *Biographies of High Monks* is a collection of biographies that was written at the beginning of the sixth century, not long after Master Tang Hôi lived.

The word *tu,* meaning Buddhist temple, was not used in Jiaozhou in the time of Master Tang Hôi. In the Preface to the *Ugradatta-paripriccha* and in *The Collection on the Six Paramitas,* while talking about the wrongdoing of people who defame the Buddha and steal precious objects from places of Buddhist practice, Master Tang Hôi uses the word *mieu* for Buddhist temple. Later on *mieu* is used to refer to Confucian shrines.

Biographies of High Monks tells us that Master Tang Hôi was of exceptional intelligence: "He was refined, eager to learn, and extremely intelligent. Not only was he knowledgeable in the Buddhist *Tripitaka,* but he was also learned in *The Six Classics*." At that time Jiaozhou was an authentic cultural center, thanks to the presence of many refugees from the north. Study and practice in the local regions naturally demanded knowledge of the two cultural bases that encountered each other in the land of Vietnam. In his writings and translations, Tang Hôi did not use the expressions and arguments of Confucianism and Taoism as Mouzi did. His writings are evidence of his fluency in Buddhism. Nevertheless, when he had to explain Buddhism to King Sun Hao, the successor of Sun Quan, he quoted from *The Book of Changes,* Zhou Gong, and Confucius. (*Biographies of High Monks* says that when he was talking with King Sun Hao he quoted the sentence: "The family that stores up wholesome deeds will have much happiness in the future.") The life and work of Tang Hôi in Dong Wu illustrates the importance of the Buddhist center in Jiaozhou that formed him. The contact between the two cultures in Jiaozhou made that country a springboard for the transmission of Buddhism to China.

National Master Thong Bien (?–1134)[1]

(Excerpt from *Flowers in the Garden of Meditation*, translated into Vietnamese by Ngo Duc Tho and Nguyen Thuy Nga, published in Hanoi, 1993)

NATIONAL TEACHER THONG BIEN of Pho Ninh Temple in the Tu Liem district was born in Dan Phuong. His family name was Ngo and his family members were all Buddhist. By nature he was intelligent and wise, and he was well-versed in the teachings of the three religions.[2]

He began to learn about the practice of meditation and received the transmission from Master Vien Chieu in the Cat Tuong Temple. After that, an imperial decree was issued summoning him to the capital, Thang Long, to be abbot of the Khai Quoc Temple. He was given the Dharma title Tri Khong. In the spring of 1096, on the full moon day of the second lunar month, Queen Phu Thanh Cam Linh Nhan (Ylan) came to the temple to offer the midday meal to the monks. While she was discussing the Dharma with the venerable elder monks she asked: "What is the meaning of Buddha and patriarch? Who is greater, who is lesser? Where is the Buddha to be found? Where do the patriarchs live? Has a patriarch ever been to our land? In the lineage of the masters after Shakyamuni Buddha, who comes first and who comes later? Who are those who, by recollecting the name of the Buddha, have realized the Dharma seal of the patriarchs?" Everyone was silent.

Master Thong Bien said: "Buddha is the one who dwells in the world and is not born and does not die. The patriarchs are those who

---

1 Formerly known as Meditation Master Tri Khong.
2 The three religions are Confucianism, Taoism, and Buddhism.

have clearly understood the Buddha mind. Their teachings and their actions go together. Only those who have not studied say wrongly that the Buddha is greater than the patriarchs or the patriarchs are greater than the Buddha. The word *Buddha* means 'awakened.' Buddha nature is beyond words, always present, and all living beings share that nature. Only because this awakened nature is covered up do living beings drift and sink according to the result of their actions and find themselves in different realms of existence. Out of compassion the Buddha appeared to be born in India, because that land is to be found at the center of the earth. At nineteen years old the Buddha left his family, and at thirty years old he realized awakening. For forty-nine years he taught the Dharma in the world. He developed different Dharma doors in order to awaken people of the world. That was the era when the Dharma arose. When he was about to pass into nirvana, fearing that people would misunderstand his meaning, the Buddha told Mañjushri: 'For forty-nine years I have not said a single word, so why do you say that I have taught the Dharma?' At that time the Buddha held up a flower by the stem. No one understood what the meaning of this was. Only the Venerable Kashyapa smiled. The Buddha knew that Kashyapa had been awakened, and he transmitted the eyes of the right Dharma to him. He was the first patriarch of the Mind school and he received the transmission without the need for scriptural teaching.[3]

"Later Kashyapa Matanga[4] brought the Buddhadharma to the Han Empire. Then Bodhidharma brought the lineage to the kingdoms of Liang and Wei. When the Dharma had been transmitted to Master

3 After the transmission had been handed down to Bodhidharma, he came to China and recited a gatha of four lines which was to become the guideline of the Meditation school in China. The meaning of the gatha is: "You do not attain the meaning of the teachings through words, since it is not transmitted from outside of your mind. The transmission goes directly from the heart of someone when they are able to see the true nature and become Buddha." The meaning of this is that the truth or reality cannot be described in words or in sutras; the teachings are just the raft taking us across the river or the finger pointing at the moon. To practice meditation is to point directly to the mind, and when you can see the true nature you are awakened, will attain the Buddha nature and become Buddha.

4 Matanga was one of two Indian monks who were the first to come to China in 68 C.E. during the reign of Han Mingdi.

Zhi Kai, the third patriarch of the Tendai school, it prospered and was called the School of the Teachings. When the lineage of Bodhidharma was transmitted to Master Hui Neng, this lineage was called the Meditation school. Both these traditions have been in Vietnam for a long time. In the Teachings school we have Mouzi and Tang Hôi. The Meditation school was first represented by the Vinitaruci school and later by the Vo Ngon Thong school." Hui Neng is the patriarch of both these schools.

The queen asked: "I don't want to say anything about the Teachings school at the moment, but is there any evidence for the two meditation schools?"

The monk replied: "According to the biography of Dharma Master Tan Qian, we are told that King Sui Gao Zu (581–604) called Master Tan Qian a Dharma instrument and told him: 'I am thinking about the path of compassion of the Awakened One, but I do not know how to repay my gratitude for it. From the throne I have supported the Three Jewels throughout the realm. I have had all the relics in the country collected and built forty-nine stupas. Abroad I have built 150 temples and stupas as an offering to help people. In foreign lands such as Jiaozhou, I have many times offered the building of stupas in order to show my gratitude and bring merit to all the worlds. Although Jiaozhou is a colony of China, it is not closely tied to us. Therefore you, Dharma master, should choose monks who are well-known for their virtue, and take them there to teach the Dharma so that all can advance on the path of awakening.'"

Dharma Master Tan Qian said: "The land of Jiaozhou has a direct link with India. When the Buddhadharma first came to Jing Dong [China] and had not been widely disseminated there, in Luy Lau there were already twenty stupas, more than five hundred monks, and fifteen sutras had been translated." Therefore the Buddhadharma came to Jiaozhou before it came to us. At that time there were monks such as Mahajivaka,[5] Tang Hôi, Kalaruci [Kalasivi],[6] and Mouzi. In our

5 An Indian monk who came to Luy Lau in the year 168–169 C.E.
6 A monk from Indoscythia, Central Asia, who came to Jiaozhou in the third century.

own time there is the Eminent Master Phap Hien, who received the transmission from Vinitaruci, who himself was the disciple of the third patriarch Seng Can. Phap Hien is a living bodhisattva who abides in the Chung Thien Temple and teaches not less than three hundred disciples, not smaller than congregations in China. His majesty the king is the kind father of the people everywhere, and wants to show equal generosity to all his subjects; therefore he intends to send monks to Jiaozhou to teach. But they already have teachers there, and we do not need to send anyone else. There is further evidence from the prime minister in the Tang era, whose name was Quan Deyu, who wrote in the preface to the book called *Transmission of the Dharma:* 'After Hui Neng passed away, the practice of meditation flourished. All the branches had successors. Meditation Master Zhangjing Yun brought the essence of the Mind school of Mazu to the lands of Wu and Nan Yue. The *mahasattva* Vo Ngon Thong brought the lineage of Baizhang to Jiaozhou and developed it there.' That is what the meditation schools have achieved in Jiaozhou."

The queen asked: "What is the order of succession in the transmission of the two meditation schools?"

The monk replied: "The Vinitaruci school at this time is represented by Lam Hue Sinh and Vuong Chan Khong. The representatives of the Vo Ngon Thong school are Mai Vien Chieu and Nhan Quang Tri. The lineage of Master Tang Hôi has Loi Ha Trach as its representative. Besides this there are many minor schools which we do not have time to mention."

The queen was very happy and bestowed on him the office of Monk Scribe, a purple *sanghati* robe, the title Great Master Thong Bien, and frequent honors and respect. Later, when the queen invited him to the palace, she made him National Teacher so that she could consult with him. Thanks to this she acquired a deep understanding of the lineage of the Meditation school. The queen wrote an insight gatha as follows:

Since form is emptiness, emptiness is form,
Since emptiness is form, form is emptiness.
When we are not caught in form and emptiness,
Then we are in harmony with the true transmission.

In old age National Teacher Thong Bien went to the Pho Ninh
Temple as abbot and gave Dharma teachings. In teaching others and
bettering himself, he often used the *Lotus Sutra*. That is why his con-
temporaries called him the Lotus Sutra Master. On the twelfth day of
the second month in the year 1134, he fell ill and passed away.

Parallax Press publishes books and tapes on mindful awareness and social responsibility. We carry all books and tapes
by Thich Nhat Hanh. For a copy of our free catalog, please
write to:

Parallax Press
P.O. Box 7355
Berkeley, California 94707
www.parallax.org

Thich Nhat Hanh has retreat communities in southwestern
France (Plum Village), Vermont (Green Mountain Dharma
Center), and California (Deer Park Monastery), where
monks, nuns, laymen, and laywomen practice the art of
mindful living. For information about retreats or local
Sanghas practicing in the tradition of Thich Nhat Hanh,
visit www.iamhome.org or write to:

Plum Village
13 Martineau
33580 Dieulivol, France
www.plumvillage.org

Green Mountain Dharma Center
P.O. Box 182
Hartland Four Corners, VT 05049

Deer Park Monastery
2499 Melru Lane
Escondido, CA 92026